The Internet

For Beginners

By Web Wise Seniors
An Educational Organization for Beginning Computer Users

TM

Web Wise Seniors, Inc.
305 Woodstock Rd.
Eastlake, Ohio 44095
www.WebWiseSeniors.com

©Copyright 2004 Web Wise Seniors, Inc.

Copyright

Trademarks

Limits of Liability/Disclaimer or Warranty

Sales Inquiries

For sales inquiries and special prices for bulk quantities, please call toll free (866) 232-7032.

Introduction

"The best computer class I have ever taken!" and "I never knew that computers could be explained so well!" are comments heard frequently from Web Wise Seniors' students. Since 2000, Web Wise Seniors has successfully taught thousands of beginning computer users. Now, for the first time, the same teaching methods successful in Web Wise Seniors' courses are found in this easy to understand book.

This book is not a reference for the Internet. It is a learning guide for people of any age who are unfamiliar with the Internet, but is especially designed for seniors who want to be skilled Internet users. It is like having a private instructor at your side as you walk through the basics of surfing the web. It is full of questions commonly asked by beginners in actual classes, followed by easily understandable answers which have already helped thousands.

You only get so far by reading explanations and definitions. You need to actually use the Internet to learn to use it well. This book will help you get started using the Internet by walking you through the basic skills Step by Step while answering your "whys" and "whats" along the way.

Web Wise Seniors teaches basic computer classes every day. WWS instructors have seen first hand what works, what does not work, and what beginners want to know. We have drawn on our teachers' knowledge, skills and experiences to write this book.

About the Authors

Web Wise Seniors is a company dedicated to teaching basic computer skills to individuals over the age of 50. Since 2000, Web Wise Seniors has filled over 22,000 classroom seats throughout Ohio, and has quickly become a premier computer education company for mature adults in the Midwest.

Classes have been designed for seniors by seniors and are continually updated with the feedback of students. By becoming an interactive part of the senior community and working closely with senior organizations throughout the Midwest, Web Wise Seniors has been able to develop a unique teaching style and curriculum that have been overwhelmingly successful.

Since 2000, over 98% of Web Wise Seniors students have stated they would recommend the program to their friends and families. One hundred percent of affiliated teaching locations have been happy to work with the WWS program and, on a 4 point scale, WWS received an average 3.77 rating in student satisfaction.*

The same dedication and love of teaching that has made the WWS program so successful in the classroom is available for you in the pages of this book. Readers will find this book full of examples, illustrations and easy to follow directions. This is a teaching guide, not just a manual or reference book.

*Student satisfaction as collected through WWS classes and events (2000 – 2005).

About this Book

The Internet for Beginners is designed to be read in order. Readers should begin with page one and continue through the book as if they were actually taking a computer course. The sections all relate and build upon each other.

Readers should keep a computer close at hand while reading ***The Internet for Beginners***. We recommend you read through an entire section and then go back and try the steps outlined in the section.

Keep a pen or pencil handy too. Take notes and highlight any sections that you feel are personally important. This is your computer book and the more personal references you make within its pages, the better this course will work for you.

Above all, please enjoy ***The Internet for Beginners***. Read at your own pace and keep at it. You'll be an Internet wiz before you know it!

Meet Larry

Larry is the Web Wise Seniors mascot. You will find him throughout the pages of this book helping to "get the bugs out." Larry has been helping beginning computer users for more than two years now. He runs the WWS help desk, answers commonly asked questions sent to www.WebWiseSeniors.com, and often makes guest appearances in WWS publications.

In his spare time, Larry enjoys searching the Internet, e-mailing friends, and belly dancing.

Acknowledgements

We would like to thank the thousands of students that have challenged our computer instructors' minds in class. Your countless, and sometimes off-the-wall, questions and constructive feedback have made us better teachers. Without you, this book would not have been possible. Thank you!

We would also like to thank our family members for their insight, feedback, and support.

Credits

Authors
Michael Douglas
Stephen Pelton

Book Design and Production
Michael Douglas
Stephen Pelton

Proof Reading
Mary Gannon
Jean Pelton
Mary Pelton

Clip Art
Microsoft 2004 Clip Art Gallery

Screen Shots
Microsoft Windows XP
Microsoft Internet Explorer

Table of Contents

Chapter 1: Let's Get Started!

Section 1: What is the Internet All About?........................ **2**

What is the Internet? **2**

History of the Internet... **3**

What can you find on the Internet?...................................... **4**

Chapter 2: Connecting to the Internet!

Section 2: Connecting to the Internet................................... **8**

Connecting to the Internet... **8**

What is a Modem?... **10**

Section 3: Selecting an Internet Service Provider **11**

Choosing an Internet Service Provider.............................. **11**

Dial-up Internet Service... **11**

Cable Internet Service... **12**

DSL: Digital Subscriber Line.. **13**

Which Type of Internet Service Do You Need?...................... **14**

What to Look for in an Internet Service Provider.................. **14**

Section 4: Internet Service Setup..................................... **15**

Easy Setup... **15**

Local Access Number... **15**

Internet Usage.. **16**

Customer Service... **17**

Choosing a Name and Password for the Internet.................. **17**

Internet Setup: Step by Step Instructions........................ **19**

Internet Setup: Visual Guide.. **20**

Table of Contents

Chapter 3: Internet Browsers!

Section 5: Opening the Internet Connection..................... **28**

What is an Internet Browser?... **28**

Opening an Internet Connection....................................... **28**

Opening an Internet Connection: Step by Step Instruction................ **28**

Opening an Internet Connection: Visual Guide…….................... **29**

How to Tell if You are Connected to the Internet......................... **31**

Section 6: Internet Browser Page Layout........................ **31**

Internet Browsers... **31**

Typical Window Layout……....….................................... **32**

File Menu.. **33**

Edit Menu... **34**

View Menu.. **34**

Favorites Menu.. **35**

Tools Menu.. **35**

Help Menu.. **35**

Toolbars.. **36**

Toolbar Buttons: Diagram.. **37**

Disconnect from the Internet.. **37**

Chapter 4: Searching the Internet!

Section 7: How to Navigate Web Pages........................ **40**

Websites and Web Pages……...................................... **40**

Hyperlinks (Links)…….. **40**

Scroll Bars.. **41**

Section 8: Website Addresses.............................. **43**

Website Addresses.. **43**

Table of Contents

What Makes Up a Typical Website Address?....................................... 44

Internal Website Pages.. 44

Websites Address vs. E-mail Address... 45

Searching the Internet.. 45

Section 9: Searching the Internet Using Website Addresses... 45

Specific Search.. 45

Specific Search: Step by Step Instructions...................................... 46

Specific Search: Visual Guide... 47

Chapter 5: Search Engines!

Section 10: Using a Search Engine.. 52

Using a Search Engine: Google.. 52

Using a Search Engine: Step by Step Instructions............................. 55

Using a Search Engine: Visual Guide... 56

Opening a Web Page from the Search Results: Step by Step Instructions.. 57

Opening a Web Page from the Search Results: Visual Guide............. 58

Moving to the Next Page of Search Results: Step by Step Instructions... 59

Moving to the Next Page of Search Results: Visual guide.................. 60

Filtering the Search Results.. 63

Filtering the Search Results: Step by Step Instructions..................... 63

Filtering the Search Results: Visual Guide..................................... 64

Search for an Exact Name or Phrase... 69

Section 11: Using the Yahoo Search Engine........................... 70

Specific Search: Step by Step Instructions...................................... 70

Specific Search: Visual Guide... 71

Using a Search Engine: Step by Step Instructions............................ 73

Using a Search Engine: Visual Guide... 73

Table of Contents

Opening a Web Page from the Search Results: Step by Step
Instructions... 75

Opening a Web Page from the Search Results: Visual Guide.............. 76

Section 12: "Page Cannot be Found" Error Message.......... 80

Chapter 6: Favorites List!

Section 13: Using the Favorites List............................ 84

Favorites/Bookmarks... 84

Add a Website to the Favorites List... 84

Add a Website to the Favorites List: Step by Step Instructions............ 85

Add a Website to the Favorites List: Visual Guide......................... 85

Using the Favorites List.. 87

Open a Favorite: Step by Step Instructions................................ 88

Open a Favorite: Visual Guide... 88

Section 14: Organizing the Favorites List...................... 90

Organizing the Favorites... 90

Organize the Favorites List: Step by Step Instructions 91

Organize the Favorites List: Visual Guide................................. 92

Opening a Favorite Located in a Favorites List Folder...................... 98

Opening a Favorite Located in a Folder: Step by Step Instructions 98

Opening a Favorite Located in a Folder: Visual Guide..................... 98

Chapter 7: History List!

Section 15: Using the History List............................... 102

Opening the History List... 103

Using the History Button: Step by Step Instructions...................... 103

Using the History Button: Visual Guide................................... 103

Table of Contents

Section 16: Erasing the History List.............................. **107**

Erasing the History List... **107**

Erasing the History List: Step by Step Instructions................ **107**

Erasing the History List: Visual Guide................................... **108**

Chapter 8: Changing the Home Page!

Section 17: Browser Home Page.............................. **114**

Changing the Home Page: Step by Step Instructions............... **115**

Changing the Home Page: Visual Guide................................ **115**

Chapter 9: Downloading & Installation!

Section 18: Downloading from the Internet.................. **120**

Adobe® Acrobat Reader... **122**

Downloading a Program from the Internet: Step by Step Instructions...... **122**

Downloading a Program from the Internet: Visual Guide.......... **123**

Section 19: Installation.. **131**

Installing New Software... **131**

The Installation Process.. **132**

Installation Process: Step by Step Instructions...................... **133**

Installation Process: Visual Guide....................................... **134**

Section 20: Opening an Installed Program.................. **140**

Opening the Program.. **140**

Open the Newly Installed Program: Step by Step Instructions............. **140**

Open the Newly Installed Program: Visual Guide................... **141**

Section 21: Removing a Desktop Icon........................ **143**

Deleting a Desktop Icon: Step by Step Instructions................ **143**

Deleting a Desktop Icon: Visual Guide................................ **144**

Table of Contents

Section 22: Downloading RealPlayer®.. **145**

RealPlayer®.. **145**

Specific Search: Step by Step Instructions........................ **146**

Specific Search: Visual Guide... **146**

Downloading from the Internet: Step by Step Instructions............ **149**

Downloading from the Internet: Visual Guide........................ **149**

Section 23: Installing RealPlayer®.. **154**

Installation Process: Step by Step Instructions...................... **155**

Installation Process: Visual Guide..................................... **155**

Setup Process: Step by Step Instructions............................. **158**

Setup Process: Visual Guide.. **159**

Chapter 10: Advertising on the Internet

Section 24: Advertising on the Internet.......................... **166**

Advertising Gimmicks.. **169**

Section 25: Internet Scams and Unwanted Advertising.... **169**

What is Phishing?... **169**

What is Adware?.. **170**

What is Spyware?... **170**

What is Sneakware?.. **170**

Eliminating Adware, Spyware and Sneakware........................ **170**

Chapter 11: Viruses!

Section 26: Viruses... **174**

What are Viruses?.. **174**

How do You get Viruses?.. **174**

What is a Trojan Horse Virus?.. **175**

What are Worms?... **175**

Table of Contents

Virus Protection... 175

Updating Windows: Step by Step Instructions....................... 176

Updating Windows: Visual Guide................................... 177

***Section 27: Firewalls*... 177**

Turning on the Windows Firewall: Step by Step Instructions.............. 178

Turning on the Windows Firewall: Visual Guide....................... 178

Chapter 12: Printing from the Internet!

***Section 28: Printing*.. 184**

The Printing Process.. 184

Printing a File (One Copy): Step by Step Instructions..................... 186

Printing a File: Visual Guide... 187

Printing a File (Multiple Copies): Step by Step Instructions.............. 188

Printing a File (Multiple Copies): Visual Guide....................... 189

***Section 29: Print Preview*... 190**

The Print Preview Option.. 190

Opening Print Preview: Step by Step Instructions...................... 191

Opening Print Preview: Visual Guide................................. 191

***Section 30: Printing Only Part of a Page*.................... 194**

The Print Selection Option... 194

Highlighting.. 194

Highlighting Your Text: Step by Step Instructions...................... 195

Highlighting Your Text: Visual Guide................................. 196

Printing a Selection: Step by Step Instructions........................ 198

Printing a Selection: Visual Guide................................... 198

Table of Contents

 Chapter 13: Saving from the Internet!

Section 31: Saving Items from the Internet........................ **202**

What Does the Term Saving Mean?.. **202**

Saving a Web Page... **203**

Locate the Example Web Page: Step by Step Instructions................. **205**

Saving a Web Page: Step by Step Instructions............................. **205**

Saving a Web Page: Visual Guide... **205**

Saving Pictures from the Internet.. **209**

Locate the Example Web Page: Step by Step Instructions................. **210**

Saving Pictures: Step by Step Instructions................................ **210**

Saving Pictures: Visual Guide... **211**

Saving Pictures (Using the Right Mouse Button): Step by Step
Instructions.. **217**

Saving Pictures (Using the Right Mouse Button): Visual Guide........... **218**

Verifying Pictures are Saved: Step by Step Instructions................. **221**

Verifying Pictures are Saved: Visual Guide............................... **222**

Saving Text from the Internet... **224**

Specific Search: Step by Step Instructions............................... **225**

Specific Search: Visual Guide.. **225**

Highlighting... **227**

Highlighting Your Text: Step by Step Instructions....................... **227**

Highlighting Your Text: Visual Guide...................................... **228**

Copying and Pasting.. **230**

Copying and Pasting: Step by Step Instructions.......................... **231**

Copying and Pasting: Visual Guide... **231**

Saving the Document.. **236**

Saving Your Work: Step by Step Instructions.............................. **236**

Saving Your Work: Visual Guide... **237**

Table of Contents

Chapter 14: Privacy on the Internet!

Section 32: Internet Privacy.. 242

Buying Products and Services Online.. 243

Chapter 15: E-mail!

Section 33: E-mail... 246

Selecting an E-mail Provider... 246

E-mail Addresses.. 247

Reading an E-mail Message.. 247

Writing an E-mail Message.. 249

Chapter 16: Internet Yellow Pages

Section 34: Internet Yellow Pages.. 254

Chapter 1

Let's Get Started!

What You Will Learn in this Chapter
- ✓ What is the Internet?
- ✓ History of the Internet.
- ✓ What can you find on the Internet?

Chapter 1: Let's Get Started!

Section 1: What is the Internet All About?

What is the Internet?

The term Internet refers to a worldwide network that connects millions of computers and their users. Through the use of phone lines, cable, and satellites, over 100 countries and tens of millions of people have the ability to communicate and share information on a global scale. The Internet has been given many names in order to try to explain its vast reach. Some of the most common terms are The Web, The World Wide Web (WWW), Cyberspace, and Information Superhighway. How did the Internet receive the name the World Wide Web? Well, if we could view the Earth in its entirety, observing all the communication lines linking the computers around the globe, the Earth would look like it was covered in a gigantic spider's web.

The Internet, or whatever term you feel comfortable using, is comprised of company, library, school, non-profit organization, and individual computers. Some computers are connected to the Internet for the purpose of sharing information and providing services, while others are connected to the Internet to search for information. Think of the Internet as a superhighway with roads connecting every destination in the World. Using your computer, you can connect to this superhighway and travel from destination to destination at almost instantaneous speed. Using computer terms, these destinations are referred to as websites and the superhighway is your Internet connection. These roads are filled with traffic consisting of people going different places. Some are performing research; some are shopping, some are communicating with friends, and others are doing everything else you can possibly imagine.

Every time you connect to the Internet, your computer is considered part of the Internet. Staying with our superhighway analogy, every computer that connects to the Internet adds to the traffic and increases the size of the Internet. When you disconnect your computer from the Internet, the size of the Internet shrinks and traffic lessens. People are constantly connecting and disconnecting to the Internet; therefore, the Internet's size is not fixed. The size of the Internet is always changing depending on the number of people who are using the Internet at any particular time.

You can travel as fast as the traffic allows on this superhighway. The time of day you connect will determine the speed at which you can travel from destination (website) to destination (website). Usually the Internet is slowest at the start of the work day, during lunch break, when the kids get out of school, just after dinner, and before bed time.

History of the Internet

The idea of linking distant locations with a network of communication lines has been around for more than a century. One of the first successful implementations of this concept was the telegraph, developed in the 1840s. The telegraph sent a signal of beeps over wires from one location to another. These signals where later standardized into Morse Code.

The Internet has come a long way since the telegraph. In 1957, the Soviet Union launched the Sputnik satellite and ignited a worldwide technological competition. In response, the US Department of Defense put together a team called the Advanced Research Projects Agency to figure out how to use its computers and technology more effectively. This group planned to link large universities, research centers, and government agencies together. The plan was to create a network of computers which could be used to share information and also become a means of communicating from one geographic area to another.

The next step was to standardize the process of sending and receiving information. In the early 1980s, a set of rules was put in place to control how the information was sent, called the TCP/IP network protocol. Also at this time, personal Desktop computer sales started to increase and the term "Internet" was coined by the Advanced Research Projects Agency.

In the early 1990s, a new standard for sending and receiving information was developed, called HTTP (Hypertext Markup Protocol). Even though the Internet was hard to use and contained mostly text information, the whole WWW system was finally made available to the public.

Chapter 1: Let's Get Started!

Marc Andreessen, a student at The University of Illinois, wanted to make the Internet easier to navigate. He created "Mosaic," a program called an Internet browser which made it easier to find information on the Internet. Mosaic also used more pictures and graphics which made it easier for the average computer user to use. Mosaic gained in popularity and Marc graduated, but since he had been a student during the program's development, the university retained the rights to Mosaic. After graduation, Andreessen started a company and, by the end of 1994, had created a new browser from scratch. He called it Netscape Navigator. By 1996, 75% of all Internet users ran Netscape Navigator on their computers.

With the success of Netscape Navigator, other companies, including Microsoft, began to realize the Internet's importance, power, and potential. Microsoft wanted to license Netscape Navigator to use with its Windows software, but Netscape refused. Therefore, Microsoft developed its own browser and called it "Internet Explorer" which hit the market in 1995 as part of the Windows program package. The rest, as they say, is history. In 1999, AOL bought Netscape, but since it didn't use it as the company's main browser, Internet Explorer became the most popular Internet browser.

What can you find on the Internet?

The Internet contains information on just about every topic imaginable. These topics include the weather, newspapers, stocks, driving directions, games, e-mail, recipes, jokes, health, nutrition, yellow pages, and much, much more. Everyday the scope of the Internet continues to grow with new businesses and people offering more information, products, and services to the public.

While people still use the Internet for research, it is not just a research tool anymore. People are using the Internet to buy and sell products and services, do research, find old friends and new romances, and as a means of communication. People from across the world are now linked together via the Internet.

It is important to realize, all the information on the Internet is *NOT* 100% accurate, true or reliable. Everything on the Internet must be looked at with a careful eye, ensuring you are receiving quality information. Anyone who has the time, basic computer skills, and wants to put forth the effort, can place information on the Internet. Have fun exploring, but be mindful of what you find.

No one person, company, or government has control of the Internet. It is a public phenomenon which has no laws, rules, or governing body. It is owned by all people all over the world. Many governments have tried to police the Internet, but since every country lives by different sets of rules and belief systems, no one system has been mandated and the rules vary from one nation to another. It is important to realize that only YOU can control what you do or the way you use and act while using the Internet. We can only hope that if we act appropriately, it will rub off on others.

Chapter 1: Let's Get Started!

Chapter 2

Connecting to the Internet!

What You Will Learn in this Chapter
- ✓ How do you connect to the Internet?
- ✓ What is a modem?
- ✓ How do you choose an Internet Service Provider?
- ✓ How do you set up Internet service?

Section 2: Connecting to the Internet

Connecting to the Internet

Now that you understand the basic structure of the Internet, you have a few choices about how to get on and use it. If you do not have a computer, you can use a company, library, or school computer to gain access to the Internet. These locations will have already paid an Internet Service Provider to allow their computers access to the Internet, so you can use their computers and get on the Internet for free. If you have your own computer, you can pay for the service yourself. This way you can use your own computer at your leisure to look around the Internet. The Internet setup process is commonly referred to as "getting connected" or "being Online."

In order to connect your computer to the Internet, you are going to need a computer with a modem, a telephone line, and an Internet Service Provider. We will discuss each of these items briefly here and then will provide additional information later in the chapter.

Most of today's computers come equipped with a piece of equipment known as a modem. The modem is a device, located inside the computer, which enables your computer to communicate with other computers. Specifically, when you connect to the Internet, the modem converts the information into a signal that can be sent across the telephone wire, like a phone call. The modem inside the receiving computer then converts the signal back into a form that the receiving computer can understand. Think of a modem as your computer's translator (English to French and then back to English) or in terms of computers (Digital to Analog and then back to Digital). Computers use a digital signal (series of 1s and 0s) whereas phone lines use an analog signal (sound wave).

Chapter 2: Connecting to the Internet!

You will also need to connect a phone line to your computer. Most people use the phone line already installed in their home, although some users will have a second phone line installed just for the computer. Using a standard telephone line to connect to the Internet is called dial-up Internet service, which is currently the most common and least expensive way to access the Internet. Other connection options, including Cable and DSL, will be discussed later in this chapter.

After purchasing a computer with a modem and hooking it up to a phone line, the last item you will need to connect to the Internet is an Internet Service Provider, also known as an ISP. For a monthly fee, an Internet Service Provider will supply you with access to the Internet. Think of the ISP as the phone service for your computer. If you went to the store and bought a new phone, you would need AT&T, Sprint, MCI or some other telecommunications company to provide you with local and long distance telephone service. The same holds true for computers. You need an ISP such as AOL, MSN, Web Wise Seniors, EarthLink, NetZero, etc. to connect you to the Internet. These companies provide you with Internet service for a fee. Basically, ISPs let your computer connect to their computer system which is in turn connected to the Internet 24 hours a day, seven days a week. ISPs are like the on-ramp to a freeway.

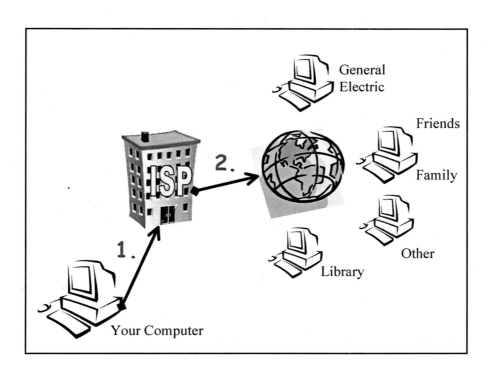

Chapter 2: Connecting to the Internet!

Once you have a computer with a modem, a phone line, and an Internet Service Provider, you can use your computer to call your Internet Service Provider to connect you to the Internet. So, put on your seatbelt, you are now ready to access to the Internet.

What is a Modem? (A Semi-Technical Description)
The word Modem is an abbreviation for Modulator-Demodulator. The purpose of a modem is to enable the computer to send information over a standard phone line. Phone lines are designed to use analog sound wave frequencies, like those created by a person talking. A computer uses a digital signal which is a series of beeps and pauses. To send the digital signal over the phone line, the modem turns these beeps into sound waves and then sends these waves across the phone line. The computer on the receiving end uses its modem to convert the analog waves back into a digital signal the computer can understand. In essence, it is the part of the computer that enables the computer to talk over the phone lines. If you do not have a modem, you cannot use the Internet.

The modem connection is typically located at the back of a desktop computer's tower (large rectangular box). On a laptop computer, the modem connection will be found on the side or the back. The modem connection looks like a phone jack. Desktop computers typically have modems with two phone jacks used to split the single wall jack between a telephone and the computer. You plug the telephone cord from the telephone into the jack with the picture of a telephone next to it. The cord from the wall jack is inserted into the opening with the picture of a phone jack next to it. As long as you are not on the Internet, you can use the telephone plugged into the computer to make or receive calls, even if the computer is turned off.

Section 3: Selecting an Internet Service Provider

Choosing an Internet Service Provider

There are a large number of Internet Service Providers (ISPs) to choose from, so let's explore some of the options available to computer users. Remember, the ultimate goal of each service is to allow you to access the Internet and everything the Internet has to offer.

The first option to look at in selecting an Internet Service Provider is how you want to connect your computer to the Internet. There are three common ways to get connected: Dial-up, Cable, and DSL service.

Dial-up Internet Service

Currently, the most popular way to access the Internet is with a Dial-Up Internet service. This type of ISP uses your standard telephone line to connect your computer to the Internet. Dial-up is the easiest way to connect to the Internet because your computer comes already setup to be connected in this fashion.

Dial-up utilizes the same principals you use when making a telephone call to a friend. You pick up the phone, dial the number, and talk when the call is answered. The only difference in connecting to the Internet is that the computer is making the call and using tones instead of words to communicate. Because your computer is using your phone line, anyone calling you will receive a busy signal while you are connected to the Internet. As soon as you disconnect from the Internet, your phone will be available for regular use.

Chapter 2: Connecting to the Internet!

Companies that provide dial-up service include AOL (America Online), MSN (Microsoft Service Network), EarthLink, NetZero, and Web Wise Seniors, just to name a few. You can find others by looking in the telephone book. The cost associated with dial-up Internet access ranges from $9.95 to $23.95 per month. (These are the common prices in effect as we write this book, but are subject to change at any time.)

Examples:
- AOL – $23.95 per month
- EarthLink - $21.95 per month
- MSN – $21.95 per month
- NetZero - $9.95 per month
- Web Wise Seniors - $19.95 per month

You are probably asking yourself, "Why should I pay different prices for the same type of service?" Typically, different companies have different supplemental services supplied with their ISP connection. The more expensive services may offer services including name recognition, national access numbers, free 24/7 customer service and, hopefully, less advertising. Many companies are able to charge less if they do not have the extra costs associated with a free 24/7 customer support line.

To set up your dial-up Internet service, it is easiest to call your ISP and have them walk you through the setup process over the phone. Before you contact the ISP, connect your computer using a phone cord to the wall phone jack. During setup, you will be typing instructions into the computer so it can contact the ISP's computer system. Once setup is complete, just open the "Internet Browser" program and the computer will automatically call to get connected to the Internet.

Cable Internet Service

Instead of just offering HBO and Showtime, many local cable companies now offer Internet Service. If you are interested in getting this type of service, call your local cable company and see if it is available in your area. How does Cable Internet Service differ from dial-up service? Well, instead of using the phone line to connect to the Internet, the computer uses your cable line. Sharing the same line will not affect your TV reception.

Chapter 2: Connecting to the Internet!

There are two advantages to Cable Internet Service. First, the cable line is able to transfer information faster than the typical phone line. Faster transfer times means that each page you look at on the Internet will load faster on your computer. Second, your phone line remains available. People will still be able to call you on the phone while you are using Cable Internet Service.

To use Cable Internet Access, the computer needs a special cable modem that you can purchase at your local electronics store. A cable modem generally runs approximately $100. The cable modem usually plugs directly into the back of the computer's tower. The new modem will allow your computer to use the cable line. Before you buy a modem, call your cable provider to determine which modem you need. After the modem is connected, call your cable company and they will walk you through the remaining steps in the setup process. Because of the increased speed and convenience of cable Internet access, the monthly charge is typically around $40.

DSL: Digital Subscriber Line

In order to respond to the high speed access being offered by the cable companies, the phone companies developed DSL Internet service. Digital Subscriber Line (DSL) Internet Service uses a telephone line specifically designed for computers. Without the burden of phone traffic, computers can transfer files and information at a faster rate. Using DSL Internet Service also leaves your phone line open for regular phone calls.

To use DSL Internet service, the computer needs a special DSL modem provided by the phone company. The DSL modem typically costs approximately $100, but many phone companies offer rebates to cover part of the cost. When you connect this new modem, it will come with instructions indicating how to connect your computer to the DSL service. Again because of this convenience, the service typically runs approximately $50 per month, and is charged directly to your phone bill. Many phone companies offer discounts on DSL service if you sign up with a year long contract.

QUESTION: What is Broadband?

ANSWER: Broadband is a term used to identify high speed Internet Access. Broadband enables a computer to transmit more data at a faster rate of speed.

Chapter 2: Connecting to the Internet!

Broadband provides enough space (bandwidth) to sufficiently carry multiple voice, video, or data channels simultaneously.

Which Type of Internet Service Do You Need?

We typically recommend new Internet users start by using standard dial-up service. This way, while you are learning, you can save money and avoid the hassle of buying the new modem. If, as you become more experienced in using the Internet, you decide you use the Internet enough to warrant the extra cost for the faster service, you can switch to one of the other Internet Services.

What to Look for in an Internet Service Provider

There are many different ways you can find an Internet Service Provider. If you prefer to use a local company, you can find a list in the standard Yellow Pages. Make sure to call a few of them to make certain you are getting a competitive price. You may also see many of the larger national services marketing their service via free CDs and computer rebates. One of the best ways to find an Internet Service Provider is to ask your friends. They will tell you if they like their service, what they pay, and whether they would use the service again.

Since you now know that many companies provide Internet Service, what should you look for in a provider?
1. Easy Setup
2. Local Access Number
3. Unlimited Usage
4. Convenient Customer Service

Section 4: Internet Service Setup

Easy Setup

One of the biggest frustrations of getting connected to the Internet is going through the setup process. The two most common ways to set up Internet service are via a CD or over the phone with a customer service representative. The CD or company representative will walk you through the steps to instruct your computer how to access the ISP's computers providing Internet access. Calling the ISP customer service department is normally the easiest way to set up your Internet service. This way, you will be speaking with a person who can answer any questions you have during the setup process.

Typically, there are three steps required to set up the computer to access the Internet. First, you will have to choose a phone number (Local Access Number) from a list provided by the ISP. This number is used to contact and connect to the ISP's computers. Second, you will select a name and password to identify yourself to your Internet Service. Third, the ISP will require you to set up your payment method.

Once the setup is complete, you can get on the Internet. Each time you tell your computer to access the Internet, the computer will dial the phone number to contact the ISP's computers. Once the computers are talking to each other, the ISP's computer will ask your computer to verify who you are. The computer will verify your name and password. After your information is verified, you will be granted access to all the resources available on the Internet.

Local Access Number

The first and most important item to consider, when using a Dial-up Internet Service Provider, is the telephone number you will use to access the Internet.

Your computer is going to make a phone call to contact the ISP's computers. If the number is not a local number, you will be charged long-distance fees during the time you are using the Internet. This can be extremely costly. If you call a local number, you will not be charged any additional fees other than your local rate.

During the setup process, the ISP will provide you with a list of phone numbers available for connecting to the Internet. It is your responsibility to choose a number from the list which is "local" to your area. By selecting the number, you are accepting responsibility for your selection. This responsibility includes any related phone charges while connected to the Internet.

QUESTION: How can you make sure you are using a local number?

ANSWER: Once you have selected a number, the only definite way to determine if the number will be a local call from your home is to contact the telephone operator. The operator will ask for your home phone number and the selected ISP number. The operator can then tell you if it will be a local call. If the operator says the call will be long distance, contact your ISP to select a different connection number.

Internet Usage

Many Internet Service Providers provide the option of either a limited or an unlimited Internet usage plan. The limited usage plan designates a specific amount of time which you can use the Internet during a month (e.g. 10 hours a month for $9.95). Any additional time exceeding your allotted time will be charged hourly. The hourly charge can be as much as $2.95 per additional hour.

The unlimited usage plan allows you to have unlimited access to the Internet for a flat monthly fee (e.g. $19.95). The unlimited usage plan is more expensive, but you do not have to track your time while you are online. Unlimited Internet usage is the most popular type of Internet usage plan.

Chapter 2: Connecting to the Internet!

Customer Service

Customer Service is a critical issue when deciding on an Internet Service Provider. Look for an ISP which provides FREE 24/7 customer service. This will allow you to get help any time you are trying to use the Internet. Be aware that some companies do not provide 24 hour service, others charge by the minute for their customer support. The charges can go as high as $2.95 per minute for help. Limiting the amount of available customer support enables companies to charge less for the Internet service, but it can cost you a great deal of time and money when you do need help.

Choosing a Name and Password for the Internet

The Internet Service Provider will require you to select a name and password during the setup process. The name and password will be used to verify who you are. This protects you from others (e.g. children) using the computer to access the Internet without your permission.

The name you are asked to select is referred to as a Username, Sign-in Name, Login Name, or Screen Name. The name can be any combination of letters and numbers, but must be unique. If you select a name that is already being used by another member of the ISP, you will be asked to choose another name.

Often people will use some combination of their first and last name when creating a username. Keep the name you choose simple because you will have to remember it to get access to the Internet. If a combination of your first and last name is not available, try using a nickname or including some numbers.

For example, someone named John Frank Doe, who was born on 1/21/1921, might choose one of the following ISP Names: DoeJ, JohnDoe, or JDoe. If those names are not available, he might try: JFDoe, DoeJF, JDoe121, etc. When you are selecting your user name, continue trying until you find one that is unique and easy for you to remember.

After selecting a username, you will be asked to choose a password. The password typically requires a minimum of 6-8 characters including both letters and numbers. Passwords are case sensitive. You will need to remember how you input the password, both capital and lower case letters, and enter it in the exact same manner every time. Choose a password you can remember, but which will be hard for others to figure out.

Chapter 2: Connecting to the Internet!

When you type in your password, do not be surprised when you see little asterisks appear instead of the actual letters or numbers. The asterisks prevent anyone around you from seeing your password as you enter it into the computer. If you think you have made a mistake while typing, erase the entire password and retype it from scratch. When setting up your password, the computer will require you to re-enter the password a second time to prevent typing mistakes. If you forget your password, you must contact your ISP to set up a new password.

QUESTION: Why must the username be unique?

ANSWER: The username must be unique because during the Internet setup process the ISP will create an electronic mailbox for you. This mailbox will allow you to send and receive messages through the computer. Your username will be the first part of your mailbox address. If two people had the same name, the mail could not be placed in the correct mailbox. Sending and receiving messages through the computer is called E-mail.

QUESTION: How is Internet service billed?

ANSWER: Internet service is typically billed to a credit card. During setup, you will be asked to provide a credit card number or your checking account information. Each month, you will automatically get charged for the service. If you want to cancel your service, you need to call the ISP and cancel before the end of the billing period. ISPs assume you are happy with their service unless you contact them.

Chapter 2: Connecting to the Internet!

Internet Service Setup: Step by Step Instructions

1. Click the START button.
2. Click the RUN option.
3. Type "inetwiz" in the input box (the white box) located on the run window.
4. Click the OK button.
   - The Internet Wizard will prompt you to select the method you want to use to connect your computer to the Internet.
5. Click the "Connect Using My Phone Line" option.
6. Click the NEXT button.
   - The Internet Wizard will prompt you to set up a new Internet account.
7. Click the "Create a New Dial-up Connection" option.
8. Click the NEXT button.
   - The Internet Wizard will prompt you to enter the phone number you dial to connect to your ISP. This number will be provided by the ISP.
   - The ISP will ask you what city and state you are calling from. It will then generate a list of local phone numbers which can be used to connect to the Internet.
9. Type the selected phone number in the designated input boxes.
10. Click the NEXT button
    - The Internet Wizard will prompt you to enter your username and password.
11. Type your username and password in the designated input boxes.
12. Click the NEXT button.
    - The Internet Wizard will prompt you to name your Internet connection.
13. Type the name of the ISP in the input box.
14. Click the NEXT button.
    - The Internet Wizard will give you the option to set up an E-mail account.
15. Click the "No" option.
16. Click the NEXT button.
17. Click the FINISH button.

Chapter 2: Connecting to the Internet!

Internet Service Setup: Visual Guide

Step 1:
Click the
START Button.

Step 2:
Click the RUN
option.

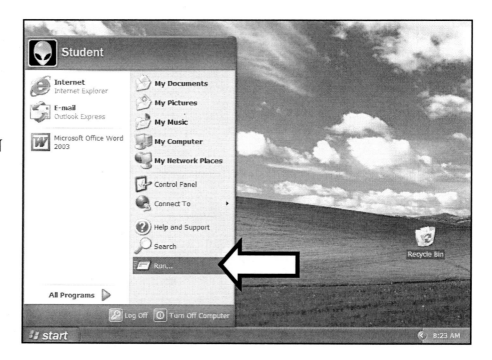

Step 3:
Type "inetwiz" in the input box located in the run window.

Step 4:
Click the OK button.

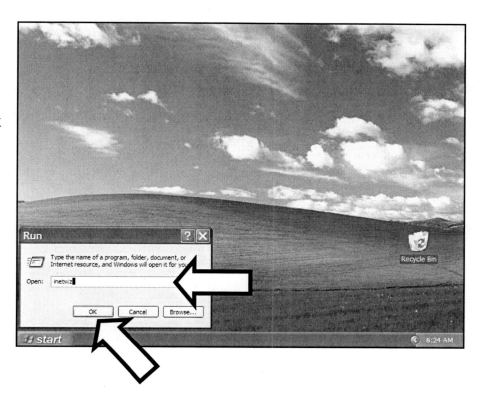

Step 5:
Click the "Connect Using My Phone Line" option.

Step 6:
Click the NEXT button.

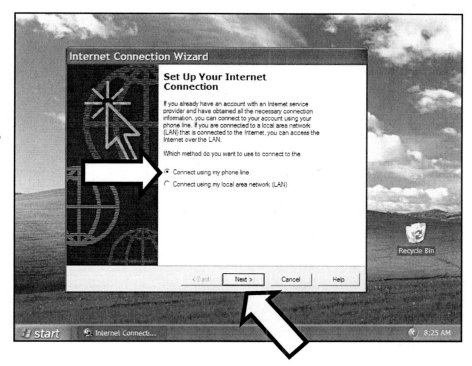

Step 7:
Click the
"Create a New
Dial-up
Connection"
option.

Step 8:
Click the NEXT
button.

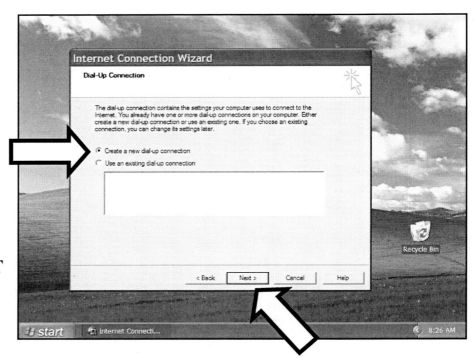

Step 9:
Type the
selected phone
number in the
designated
input boxes.

Step 10:
Click the NEXT
button.

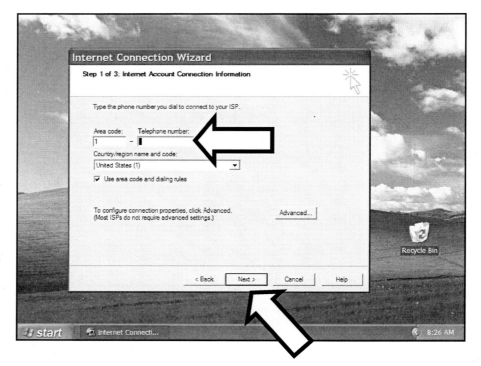

Step 11:
Type the username and password in the designated input boxes.

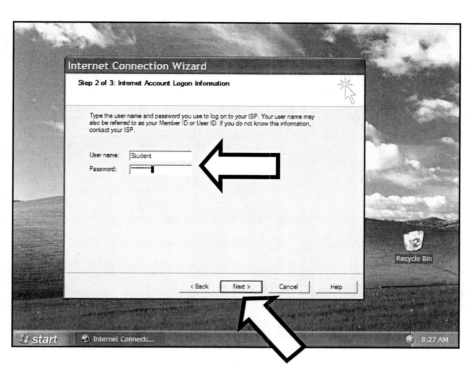

Step 12:
Click the NEXT button.

Step 13:
Type the name of the ISP in the input box.

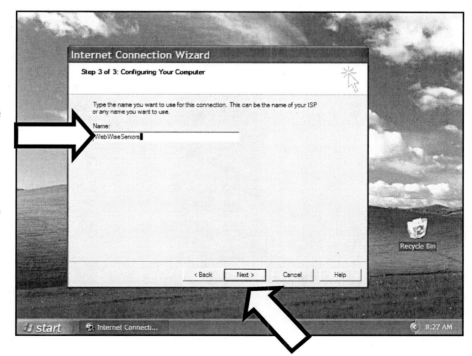

Step 14:
Click the NEXT button.

Step 15:
Click the "No"
option.

Step 16:
Click the NEXT
button.

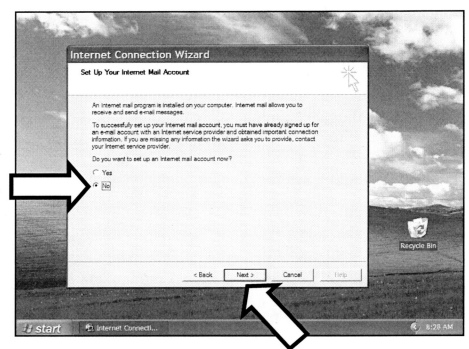

Step 17:
Click the
FINISH button.

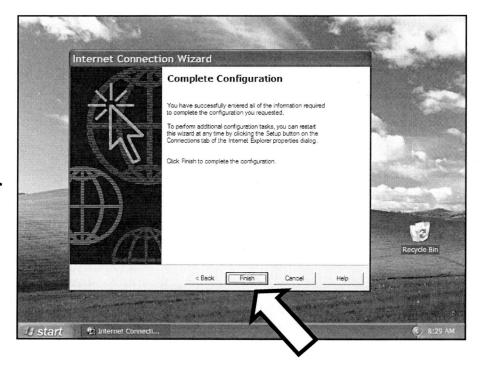

Chapter 2: Connecting to the Internet!

QUESTION: Does the Internet Service Provider you choose restrict your access to the Internet?

ANSWER: Once you are connected to the Internet, you are not limited to the information you can see or use. There are specific sites that require a fee to use their resources, but this has nothing to do with your ISP. Therefore, it does not matter which company you choose as an Internet Service provider; each one acts as a doorway to the same place. Once you are inside, you have access to the same things available to others using a different Internet Service Provider.

Take a moment to think of the Internet as a local shopping mall. When you drive into the parking lot, you have many doors to choose from to gain access to the inside of the mall. The doors are the ISP and the Internet is the mall. It does not matter which door you use, because once you are inside, you will be able to enter all of the available stores. The same is true for the Internet.

QUESTION: If you are on the Internet, anyone who calls will get a busy signal. Is there any way to get around this?

ANSWER: If you are connected to the Internet using a dialup Internet Service, anyone trying to call you will get a busy signal. The busy signal is the result of your computer sending and receiving information via the phone line. To fix this problem consider one the following solutions.

First, you could consider having a second phone line installed in your home; one for the computer and the other for regular phone calls. Second, you could set up a voice mail account with your phone company. This way, a person can leave a message which you can access when you are finished using the computer. Third, you could use a different type of Internet service like DSL or cable. These services do not tie up your phone line. Fourth, there are programs which will alert you if you are receiving an incoming call. These programs normally will display the name and number of the caller plus give you an option of taking the call. These programs vary in price and can be found on the Internet (e.g. Callwave.com and buzzme.com).

Chapter 2: Connecting to the Internet!

Chapter 3

Internet Browsers!

What You Will Learn in this Chapter
- ✓ What is an Internet Browser?
- ✓ How do you open an Internet Connection?
- ✓ Window and Browser layout.
- ✓ Browser menu options.
- ✓ Toolbar functions.

Section 5: Opening the Internet Connection

What is an Internet Browser?

A browser is a program which enables the computer to display the text and graphics located on the Internet. The Internet consists of billions of pages of information, pictures, text, animations, etc. A page on the Internet is called a web page. A group of web pages provide by one company is called a web site.

All of these web pages are built using computer code which tells the computer how to display the text and graphics. The computer code is called HTML (Hypertext Markup Language). The browser translates the computer code and converts the code into graphical pages. A browser is nothing more than a program used to display web sites and help you navigate around the Internet. It translates each web page from computer language into something people can understand. Internet Explorer and Netscape are two examples of browsers.

Opening the Internet Connection

When an Internet browser is opened, the computer will automatically attempt to connect to the Internet. The browser will instruct your computer to use the Internet connection which was setup with your ISP. Assuming you are using a Dial-up Internet service, the computer will open a window which can be used to start the connection. After pressing the "Connect" button, the computer will dial the phone number to connect you to the ISP's computers. When a successful connection is established, the connection window will disappear and the browser will display your first Internet page. Getting connected to an ISP's computers is called "signing on" or "logging on."

Opening an Internet Connection: Step by Step Instructions
1. **Click the "START" button.**
2. **Choose your browser from the list. (Ex. INTERNET EXPLORER)**
3. **Click your left mouse button.**
4. **Click the "CONNECT" button located on the Connection Window.**

Opening an Internet Connection: Visual Guide

**Step 1:
Click the
"START"
button.**

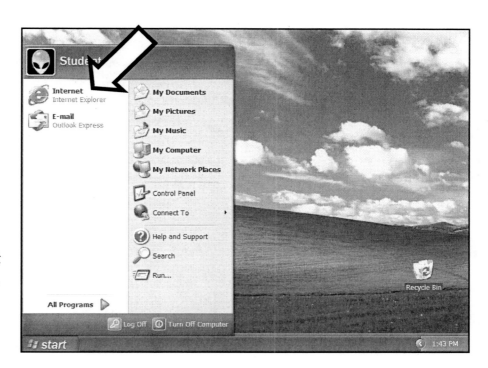

**Step 2:
Choose your
browser.
(Ex. Internet
Explorer)**

**Step 3:
Click your left
mouse button.**

**Step 4:
Click the
"CONNECT"
button located
on the
Connection
Window**

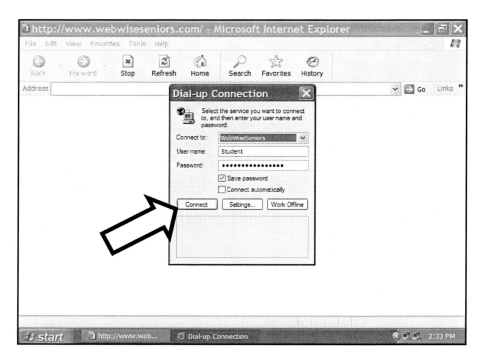

**A web page will
be displayed in
the browser
window when
the connection
is established.**

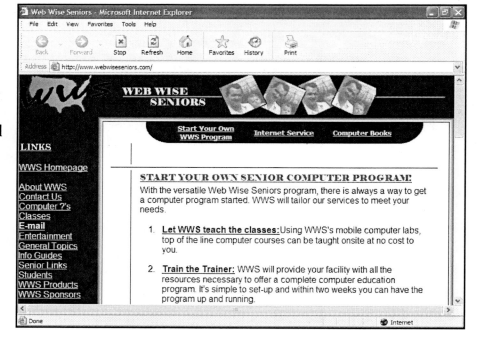

How to Tell if You are Connected to the Internet.

You can tell when a computer is connected to the Internet in two ways. If you look in the blue taskbar in the bottom right hand corner of the screen, you will see the computer's clock. Once you are connected to the Internet, there will be a picture of two small blinking computer monitors found next to the clock. When you disconnect from the Internet, the picture of two monitors will disappear.

The second way to tell if you are connected to the Internet is to look at the browser. If you open the file menu in Internet Explorer, there will be an option which says "offline." If the computer is not connected to the Internet, there will be a check mark next to the Offline option.

Section 6: Internet Browser Page Layout

Internet Browsers

All browsers perform the same basic function. They display web pages and provide tools to aid in the navigation of the Internet. When you become familiar with one browser, you should feel confident that you can use the other browsers. The screen layout, navigation buttons, and features are similar in each browser. Internet Explorer is currently the most popular Internet browser. It gained popularity because it comes standard on all computers running Windows. Other popular browsers are Netscape, Opera, and Mozilla Throughout the remainder of the book we will use Internet Explorer as our example browser.

When a person is looking around the Internet, they are said to be "Browsing" or "Surfing." Located near the top of the browser window is the menu bar, which allows you to make choices about what to do when you are on the Internet. Underneath the menu bar is the toolbar, which contains buttons which help navigate the Internet. The navigation buttons include Back, Forward, Stop, Refresh/Reload, and Home. Each button plays an important role in making sure you do not get lost while searching the Internet.

Other features of the Internet browser include the Address line, Favorites list and History list. The Address line provides you with a location to type in the address of a website. The Favorites list enables you to save addresses of websites, and the History list keeps track of what websites you visit while you are using the Internet. These items will be discussed more as we get started using the Internet.

Notice that once Internet Explorer was opened and your Internet connection was established, the browser automatically showed a web page. This starting page is referred to as your Home Page. Typically, during setup, the computer's Home Page is set to your ISP's main web page. As you become comfortable using the Internet, you will be able to change your Home Page.

Typical Window Layout

Most programs, including Internet Explorer, open in a box called a "window." Every window has certain characteristics: the title bar, Minimize button, Maximize button, Close button, menu bar, the tool bar, and the task bar.

The title bar is located at the top of every window. The title bar displays the name of the program opened in the window. The task bar located at the very bottom of the screen will display a button corresponding to each open window. The task bar button will have the same name as the window's title bar.

The Minimize, Maximize/Restore and Close buttons are located on the right side of the title bar. The minimize button has a picture of a minus sign in it. Minimize removes the window from the screen, but does not close it. Your information is not lost, just hidden. When you minimize a window, the window is stored on your taskbar at the bottom of the screen. To retrieve your window, simply place your mouse arrow on the button that represents the minimized window and press the left mouse button once. The window will reappear on the computer screen.

The maximize button is the middle button. This button has a picture of a big square on it. When you press the Maximize button, your window will stretch to cover the entire computer screen. After a window has been maximized, the large square box turns into two small squares. This change occurs to tell you that the window is at its maximum size. This button is now called the Restore button. If you click the maximize button again, the window will restore itself to its original, smaller, size.

The close button is located in the far right corner of each window. The close button is typically red with a large white "X" on it. The close button removes the window from the computer screen, removes the window's button from the taskbar, and turns off the program. Unsaved information will be lost.

The menu bar is located directly beneath the title bar. The menu bar contains options that will affect information displayed in the window. The Internet Explorer window you are working with has six menus: FILE, EDIT, VIEW, FAVORITES, TOOLS and HELP.

File Menu

The File menu controls the main options available through the browser. The most important items in the File menu are the Save and Print options, but we've included a brief description of each option below.

New – Used to open a new browser screen.
Open – Provides an input box to type in a website address or file location, which will then be displayed in the browser window.
Edit with Microsoft Word – Opens a web page in Microsoft Word for editing purposes.
Save As – Saves the current web page and its contents to your computer.
Page Setup – Allows users to change how web pages are displayed and printed. Vertical (portrait) vs. horizontal (landscape). It also allows you to change page margins.
Print – Opens the print dialog window allowing you to select the desired number of copies and print range.

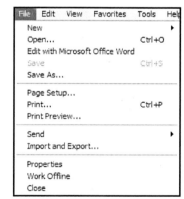

Print Preview – Displays the web page as it will look on paper.
Send – Used to send the current web page or a link to the current web page through e-mail. This feature requires the use of Microsoft Outlook or Outlook Express.
Import and Export – Used to update the computer's Favorites list, if another Internet browser was used in the past.
Properties – Provides details about the current web page.

Work Offline – Allows you to use the browser when the computer is not connected to the Internet. A check mark will be present next to this option if you are viewing a website, but are not connected to the Internet.

Close – Closes the browser window.

Edit Menu

The Edit menu provides options to copy or find an item on a web page.

Copy – Allows you to copy a highlighted section of a web page.

Cut – Allows you to copy a highlighted section of a web page. Only the person in charge of the webpage (the webmaster) can remove or edit a live web page.

Paste – Allows you to paste text which has been copied from a web page.

Select All – Highlights the entire contents of the web page.

Find – Opens an input box to locate a specific word(s) on the current web page.

View Menu

The View menu changes the way the browser displays a web page. It also provides options to change the browser toolbar settings.

Toolbars – Lists alternative buttons that can be displayed on the toolbar.

Status Bar – On/off switch for the gray bar located at the bottom of the browser window displaying links. The status bar displays a progress bar while a web page is loading.

Explorer Bar – Splits the main screen into two sections providing space to display the Favorite, History, and Folder lists.

Go To – Provides options for web site navigation.

Stop – Halts a web page from loading into the browser.

Refresh – Reloads a web page.

Text Size – Increases or decreases the size of the web site text.

Encoding – Instructs the browser as to what language to use when decoding the web page.

Source – Displays the HTML code used to create the web page.

Privacy Report – Lists any restrictions placed on the current web page by your privacy setting on Internet Explorer.

Chapter 3: Internet Browsers!

Full Screen – Displays the web page using the entire computer screen. This limits the menu options and navigation tools.

Java Console – Enables Internet Explorer to use Java in the HTML web page code.

Favorites Menu

The Favorites Menu provides a list of web pages which have been saved to your Favorites list. The menu displays the list and includes options for adding new web pages and organizing the current list.

Add to Favorites – Opens a new window allowing you to add the current web page to your Favorites list.

Organize Favorites – Provide options to organize your Favorites list including Create Folders, Rename, and Delete.

Tools Menu

The Tools Menu contains features which change how the browser works.

Mail and News – Provides options for automatically opening your e-mail program in order to send or read messages.

Synchronize – If a web page is set to be displayed offline, the computer automatically checks to make sure the computer has the most current copy of the web page.

Windows Update – Tells the computer to check for any updates to the browser program provided by the manufacturer.

Messenger – Launches the Microsoft Instant Messenger program.

Internet Options – Opens a list of options which can affect how the browser displays web pages. These options include privacy policies, connection setting, and your Home Page.

Help Menu

The last menu in Internet Explorer is the Help Menu. The Help Menu provides resources to help you use the browser program. The Help feature has definitions and instructions to help perform basic tasks when using the browser program.

Chapter 3: Internet Browsers!

Toolbars

The toolbar buttons are the primary tools of Internet Explorer. To perform the given task, click once on a toolbar button. Clicking twice instructs the computer to perform the task two times. The toolbar buttons are used primarily to navigate around the Internet. If the toolbar button is light gray, the option is not available.

1. **Back Button** – Returns you to the screen you were viewing before the current one.

2. **Forward Button** – Takes you to the screen you were viewing before you clicked the **Back** button.

3. **Stop Button** – Temporarily stops your computer from transferring information from the Internet. Useful when errors are discovered or you have reached the wrong site.

4. **Refresh Button** – Reloads the web site you are currently viewing.

5. **Home Button** – Takes you to your Starting Page.

6. **Favorites Button** – Allows you to save a web site address on your computer for future access.

7. **History Button** – Shows you a list of the web pages you have viewed.

8. **Print Button** – Prints the page currently being displayed on screen.

9. **Address Bar** – Contains the exact web address of the web site you are currently viewing.
   - For example: www.webwiseseniors.com

Chapter 3: Internet Browsers!

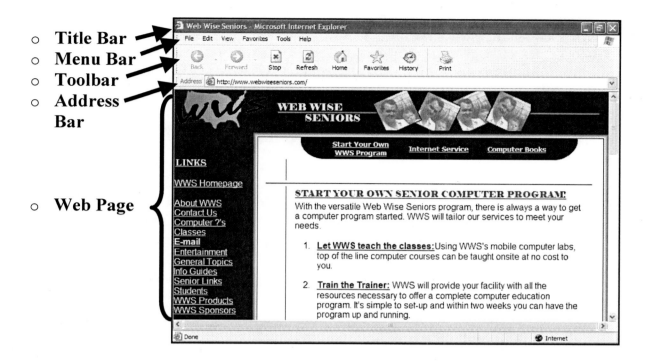

- ○ **Title Bar**
- ○ **Menu Bar**
- ○ **Toolbar**
- ○ **Address Bar**
- ○ **Web Page**

Toolbar Buttons: Diagram

Back   Forward   Home   History   Print

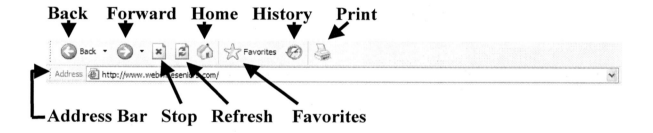

Address Bar   Stop   Refresh   Favorites

Disconnect from the Internet

When you are finished using the Internet, simply close the browser window. The computer should automatically ask if you would like to disconnect from the Internet. Select the Disconnect option and your computer will stop transferring data. Stopping the Internet connection is referred to as Logging Off or Signing Off.

QUESTION: I do not want to use Internet Explorer. How do I find a different browser?

ANSWER: If your computer is running Windows, Internet Explorer is probably already loaded on your computer. If you decide you would like to use a different Internet browser, go to www.download.com. You can find different browsers there.

QUESTION: What if the computer does not automatically display the disconnect message window?

ANSWER: Move your mouse down to the symbol of the two blinking monitors found in the lower right corner of the screen. After the mouse pointer is positioned over the image, click the right mouse button. A list of options will appear. Place your mouse pointer over the disconnect option and click the left mouse button. This will force the computer to stop communications with your ISP's computers.

Chapter 4

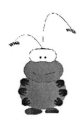

Searching the Internet!

What You Will Learn in this Chapter
✓ How do you navigate web pages?
✓ What makes up a typical web site address?
✓ How is a website address different from an e-mail address?
✓ How do you search the Internet using a website address?

Section 7: How to Navigate Web Pages

Websites and Web Pages

A website is similar to a "choose your own adventure" book. You begin reading from the first page, commonly referred to as the Home Page. The first page will have many choices (called hyperlinks or links) which will take you to subsequent pages in the website.

Hyperlinks (Links)

A hyperlink (which is commonly shortened to link) is often a picture, word, or a set of words which will take you to a new web page. Links are usually blue underlined text, although they can be any color. Web pages typically have many links on each page. Using your mouse, click your left mouse button on a link. This will take you directly to the chosen page.

How do you know what is a link and what is not? When the mouse pointer is placed over a link, the mouse pointer will change from an arrow into a hand. The hand symbol indicates that clicking on the text or picture (the link) will take you to a new web page.

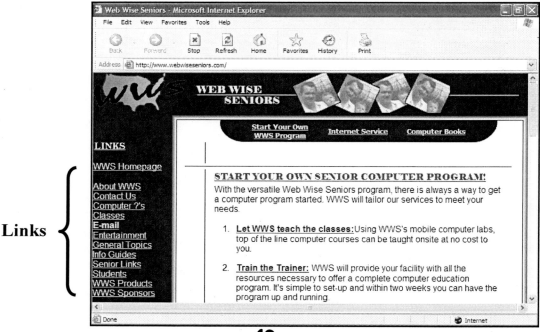

Chapter 4: Searching the Internet!

Scroll Bars

Web pages are laid out in the same vertical fashion as ancient Egyptian scrolls. Therefore, there is often information located above and/or below your computer screen. To see all the available information on the page, use the vertical scroll bar located on the far right side of the window screen.

The scroll bar is made up of an arrow pointing up, an arrow pointing down, and a bluish-gray button in the middle. Clicking on the up and down arrows at the top and bottom of the scroll bar moves the information on your screen. Each click on the up arrow will move your viewing screen one line up your page. Each click on the down arrow will move your viewing screen one line down the page.

The button located within the scroll bar tells you where you are in relation to the total information available for viewing on the computer screen. If the button is at the top of the scroll bar, you are at the beginning of the information. If the button is at the bottom of the scroll bar, you are at the end of the information. Notice that when you press the up arrow, the button moves up the screen. When you press the down arrow, the button moves down the screen. If you press either the up or down arrow and nothing happens, you may already be at the top or bottom of the document. To see if this is the case, check to see if the button is at the top or bottom of the scroll bar.

HINT: Put your mouse arrow on either the up or down arrow. Press and hold the left mouse button down. As long as you hold the button down, you will continue scrolling up/down your document. This comes in handy when scrolling through a long document.

HINT: Another way to scroll includes the "clicking and dragging" method. Place your mouse arrow on top of the bluish-gray button in the middle of the scroll bar. Press and hold down the left mouse button. While holding down the left mouse button, move your mouse arrow up and down the screen. This "clicks and drags" the button through the scroll bar enabling you to scroll through your web page very quickly.

Chapter 4: Searching the Internet!

Practice using the scroll bar with the up and down arrows. Also practice clicking and dragging the bluish-gray button in the middle of the scroll bar.

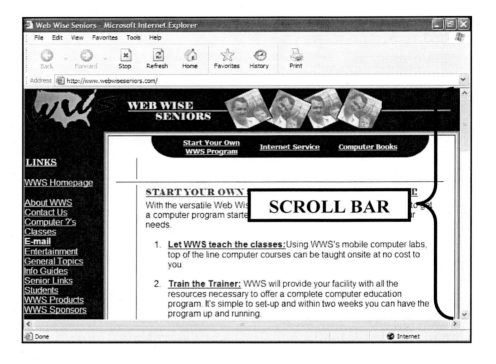

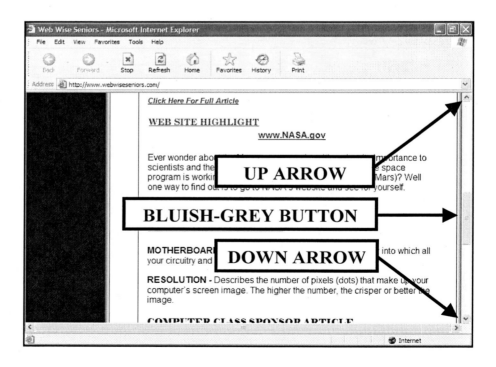

Section 8: Website Addresses

Website Addresses

Every website on the Internet has a unique address telling the computer where that website is located. A website address typically has three parts. The first part indicates that the website is part of the World Wide Web. World Wide Web is abbreviated with three w's followed by a period (www.). The second part of a website address is the name of the website. The name can be one word, a few letters or numbers, or a series of words grouped together. The only requirement for a website name is that it cannot contain any spaces. The third and final part of an address is the "extension" at the end of the name. The most common ending is .com, but others include .edu, .gov, .net, .org, etc. The combination of the website name and the extension is unique. No other website on the Internet will have the same name and extension. If two websites had the same address, the computer would not know from where to retrieve the information.

A website address is very similar to a house address. Each home address starts with a number followed by a street name. Each house address is different from the other houses on the street. This makes it possible for people to locate the house and for the postal worker to deliver the mail.

As the Internet grows, companies have a harder time selecting unique website addresses. As a result, companies started registering used names with different extensions to make them unique. In the beginning, the extension used to indicate the type of website. .com stood for commercial companies, .org for non-profit agencies, .edu for schools, and .gov for government sites. But, as time went on, companies and individuals began registering names and extensions, regardless of affiliation, so long as the address was not already taken. This has made the extension almost meaningless in signifying website types.

Chapter 4: Searching the Internet!

HINT: Website addresses may not contain any spaces. They are not case sensitive.

What Makes Up a Typical Web Site Address?

Examples: www.WebWiseSeniors.com, www.google.com, www.whitehouse.gov, www.yahoo.com

Part 1: www.
- o **www** stands for World Wide Web

Part 2: Name
- o May **NOT** contain any spaces
- o Web Addresses are **NOT** case sensitive

Part 3: Extension
- o (.com , .gov , .net , .org , .edu, or .cc)

A website address is a direct link to a website. By typing the address into the Internet browser, you are telling the computer to go directly to the desired website. Website addresses can be obtained from television, radio, newspapers, and friends.

Internal Website Pages

A website has many pages within the site. Books are divided into chapters. Well, websites are divided into folders. The specific address for an internal webpage begins with the website address, followed by the folder name, followed by the page name. Each part is separated by a forward slash.

If we use the example, **www.usatoday.com/travel/front.htm,** we see the first part of the address is the website address www.usatoday.com. Typing the website address will open the Home Page of the website. The "/travel/" indicates that the page is located in the travel folder (section) of the website. The third part, "front.htm" is the page name. It is important to type in the exact address or the computer will not be able to find the page and will display a "page not found" error message.

Website Address vs. E-mail Address:

A website address is different from an e-mail address. E-mail addresses must include the @ ("At") symbol. E-mail addresses are used to send and receive messages to individuals over the Internet.

Example website address: www.webwiseseniors.com
Example e-mail address: johndoe@webwiseseniors.com

Searching the Internet

There are two ways to search the Internet. The first way is by conducting a specific search which is accomplished by typing a website address into your browser and going directly to a site. This method is only possible if you know the website address of the site you are interested in viewing. The second way to search through what the Internet has to offer is with a search engine. A search engine is the card catalog system of the Internet. You can type in a topic and the search engine will generate a list of websites that deal with that topic.

Section 9: Searching the Internet Using Website Addresses

Specific Search

Located near the top of the Internet browser window is the address bar containing a white input box. The address bar is used to display the address of the website currently being viewed in the browser window. You can also use it to open a website by conducting what is referred to as a specific search. To proceed with a specific search, you need to know the exact address of a website or web page.

Chapter 4: Searching the Internet!

To attempt a specific search, you need the website address and a blank address bar. To type in the address bar, move your mouse pointer over any part of the white input box. Click the left mouse button once. Everything in the input box should turn blue (becomes highlighted). When something turns blue, it indicates that the computer is looking at it and waiting for further instructions. Use the backspace key or the delete key on the keyboard to erase the highlighted text. Begin typing the new website address.

If you click the left mouse button in the address line and everything does not turn blue, you will have to erase the text manually. A blinking line (cursor) should be located in the address bar. The cursor will appear at the point in which you clicked the mouse. Use the backspace key on the keyboard to erase to the left of the cursor and the delete key to erase the text to the right. After the text has been completely erased from the input box, type in the new website address.

Be careful to be exact when typing in the new website address. If any mistakes are made, the computer will not be able to find the correct page. When you are finished typing, either hit the Enter key on your keyboard or move your cursor over the "Go" button located at the end of the address line and click your left mouse button.

Specific Search: Step by Step Instructions

1. Obtain a website address from the TV, radio, newspaper, or friend.
2. Position the mouse pointer over the input box located in the address line.
3. Click the left mouse button one time.
4. Press the backspace key or the delete key on the keyboard to erase the highlighted text.
5. Type the new website address in the input box.
   - Remember a website address typically includes:
     o www. followed by
     o The unique name, followed by
     o The extension (.com , .gov , .net , .org , .edu or .cc)
       ▪ Example: www.WebWiseSeniors.com
6. Press the Enter Key on your keyboard to go to the website.

Chapter 4: Searching the Internet!

Specific Search: Visual Guide

Step 1:
Obtain a website address from the TV, radio, newspaper, or friend.

Step 2:
Position the mouse pointer over the input box located in the address line.

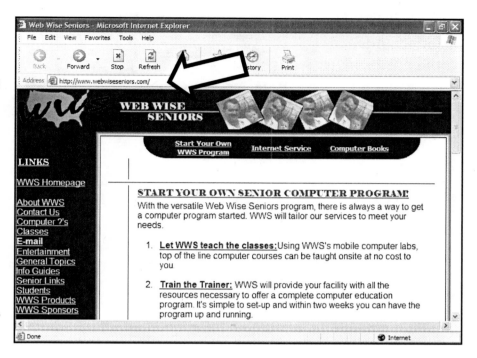

Step 3:
Click the left mouse button one time.

Step 4:
Press the backspace key or the delete key on the keyboard to erase the highlighted text.

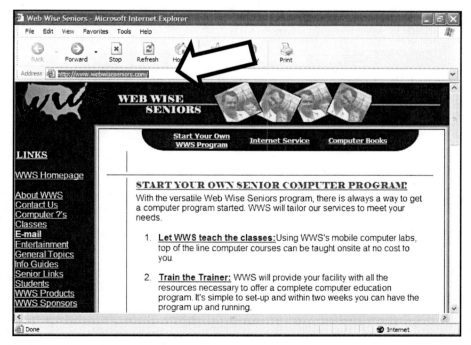

Step 5:
Type the new
website address
in the input box.

Step 6:
Press the Enter
Key on your
keyboard to go
to the website.

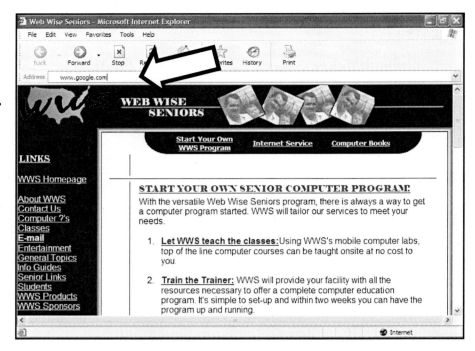

Result of the
specific search.

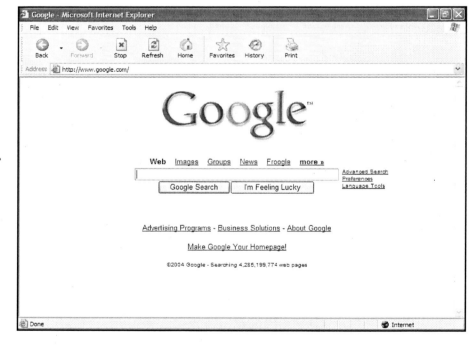

For practice, repeat the steps of the specific search using the website addresses located in the Internet Yellow Pages in Chapter 16.

QUESTION: What does the HTTP:// represent?

ANSWER: Take a moment to examine the address line. The computer automatically adds "http://" before the website address. Technically these letters stand for Hypertext Transfer Protocol. Basically, it enables the computer to transfer hypertext files (files containing links) across the Internet. There are other protocols, but HTTP is the most commonly used protocol on the World Wide Web. You do not need to type in these letters. Your Internet browser knows they are supposed to be there and will put them in for you.

Chapter 4: Searching the Internet!

Chapter 5

Search Engines!

What You Will Learn in this Chapter
✓ What is a search engine?
✓ How do you use a search engine?
✓ How do you open a web page in the search engine results?
✓ How do you filter the search results?
✓ How do you search the Internet using an exact name or phrase?
✓ How do you use the Yahoo search engine?
✓ Why do you get the "Page Cannot Be Found" error message?

Section 10: Using a Search Engine

A search engine is the second, and often the most productive, way to locate information on the Internet. A search engine is a website that acts like a card catalog (database) of the Internet. After you type a topic (word or group of words) into a search engine, it generates a list of websites pertaining to the topic. The list includes a brief description and a link to each of the websites.

There are many search engines available on the Internet. Currently, the most popular are Google and Yahoo. Search engines gain popularity for many reasons including the number of cataloged websites, accuracy, speed of results, and ease of use.

Google has more than four billion web pages in its database and each is categorized by topic. Google produces results that match your search terms or close variations of the words entered. Google then ranks each page using the number of external links pointing to the page from other websites and also by seeing the page relates to your search topic. Pages with the highest rank will be displayed first in the results list, and so on. When looking through the list, read the web page summaries taken directly from the text on the web page. This will save time and ensure that the page has the information you want.

Using a Search Engine: Google
The first step in using a search engine is to go to a search engine website. Open your Internet browser and type the website address into the address line. When you have finished typing, press the Enter button located on the keyboard. The search engine will be displayed in the browser window. In this example, you will be using Google's search engine. Google's website address is www.google.com.

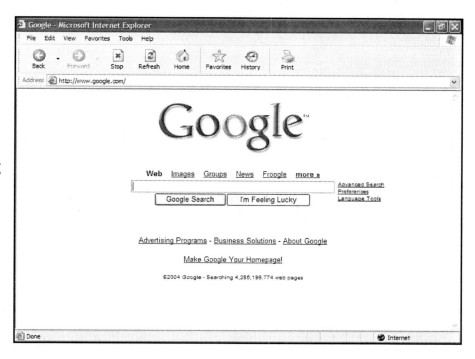

The Google Search Engine Starting Page.

There will be a white input box on Google's starting page (Home Page). This input box, called the search bar, is used to enter the search term(s). Before you begin typing, the search bar must be activated. The activated bar will display a black blinking line (cursor) on the left-hand side. If the cursor (blinking line) is not present, position your mouse pointer over the white input box and click the left mouse button. The cursor will appear in the input box. Using the keyboard, type in the subject on which you want information. In this example, type in the word "nutrition." Once you have finished typing, either press the Enter key on the keyboard or click your left mouse button on the "Google Search" button located directly below the search input box. The search engine will generate a list of websites relating to nutrition.

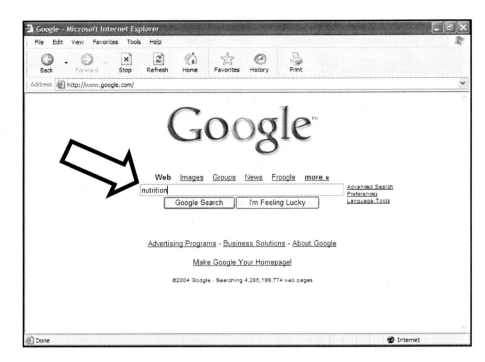

Search Input Box.

Let's analyze the resulting page. Located at the top of the page, is a search box displaying the topic you entered. A second search box is located at the very bottom of the page, enabling you to enter additional terms or to begin a new search. Below the search box is a blue line displaying information on what the Google's search has accomplished. The left side of the line tells you Google searched the web for your subject. The right side displays the number of results found. Results one through ten are displayed on the current page, while the remainder (more than 20 million) will be listed on the following pages. If you cannot find a web page offering the desired information in the first few result pages, you need to focus (filter) the list. On the far right side of the blue bar, you will notice that Google takes a moment to brag how quickly (less than one second!) it found the results of your search.

Search Input Box.

Blue Results Line.

Web Page List.

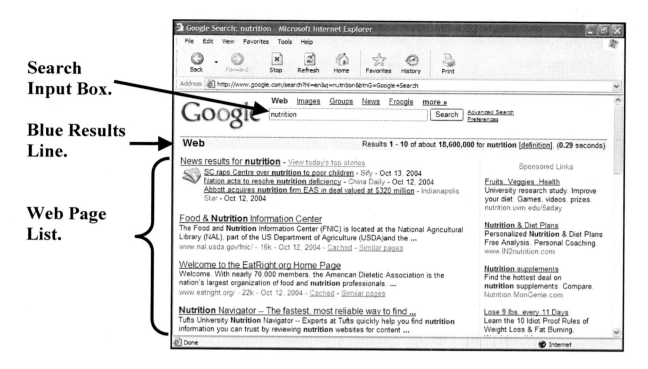

Using a Search Engine: Step by Step Instructions

1. Open the search engine website (www.google.com).
2. Type the search term(s) into the input box provided.
3. Press the Enter key on the keyboard or click the GOOGLE SEARCH button.
    -   Other search engines call the Search button the Find, Fetch, or Go button.

Chapter 5: Search Engines!

Using a Search Engine: Visual Guide

Step 1:
Open the search engine website.

(www.google.com)

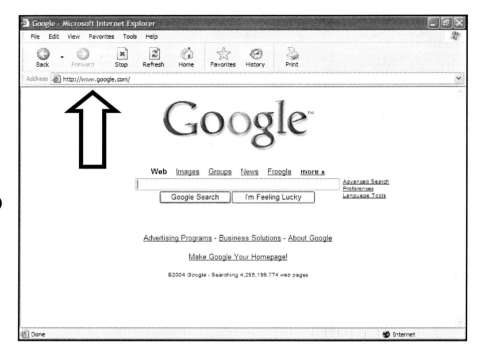

Step 2:
Type the search term(s) into the input box provided.

Step 3:
Press the Enter key on the keyboard or click the GOOGLE SEARCH button located on the screen.

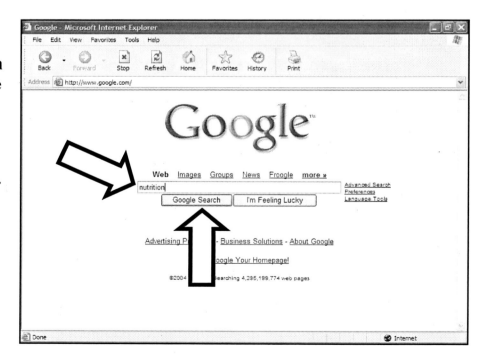

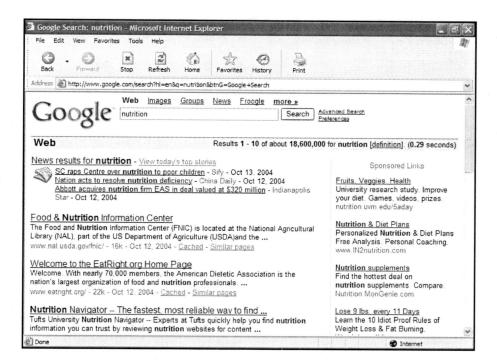

Search results page.

Below the blue line, the first ten websites will be listed. Each listing will include a description, the web page address, and a link to the page. The link is the top line of the listing (the blue underlined words). Move the mouse pointer over the link and the pointer will change from an arrow into a hand. Remember this is the browser's way of indicating a link. Click on the link and the web page will be displayed in the browser window.

Note: The list displayed on the far right side of the screen is a list of advertisers. These companies enable the public to use the search engine for free.

Opening a Web Page from the Search Results:
Step by Step Instructions

1. **Move the mouse pointer over the link (blue underlined words).**
   - **The pointer will change from an arrow into a hand.**
2. **Click on the link using the left mouse button.**
   - **The web page will be displayed in the browser window.**

Chapter 5: Search Engines!

Opening a Web Page from the Search Results: Visual Guide

Step 1:
Move the mouse pointer over the link.

Step 2:
Click on the link using the left mouse button.

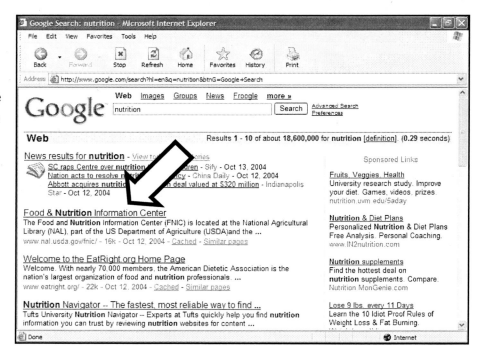

Open Web Page.

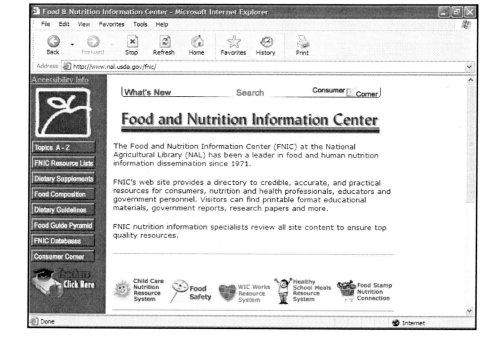

Chapter 5: Search Engines!

Once you have viewed a web page from the Google search list, you might want to go back to the results list and choose another website link. Use the Back button located on the browser toolbar to return to the page you came from. Each time the Back button is selected (clicked) using the mouse, the browser moves back one page. Depending on how deeply you have navigated into the website via the page links, you may need to click the Back button several times. Use the Back button to return to the Google search list. If you inadvertently go back too far, use the Forward button to move forward to the page you just returned from.

Using the scroll bar located on the right-hand side of the browser window, scroll down the results page to view the other web pages in the list. Remember, to use the down scroll, position your mouse over the down arrow beneath the scroll bar and click the left mouse button. Each time you click, the browser will move down one line on the page. For practice, open another web page from the list, view the web page and then use the back button to return to the Google list. Scroll down the results page until you reach the bottom.

The first Google search results page displays the first ten web pages. To move to the next page of results, displaying results 11 through 20, use the "Next" link located to the right of the "Goooooogle" image. Notice the "Goooooogle" image has numbers located under the letters of the image. These numbers can be selected to move directly to the specific pages of results. Practice moving to the next few results pages. Try opening a few more web pages.

Moving to the Next Page of Search Results:
Step by Step Instructions
1. **Scroll down to the bottom of the results page.**
2. **Click the NEXT link or**
   - **Click the page numbers located beneath the "Goooooogle" image.**

Moving to the Next Page of Search Results: Visual Guide

Step 1:
Scroll down to the bottom of the results page.

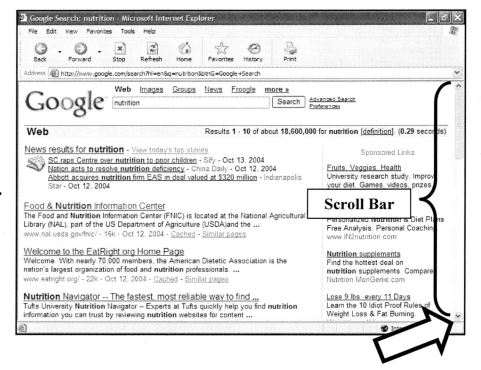

Continue scrolling down the results page until you reach the bottom.

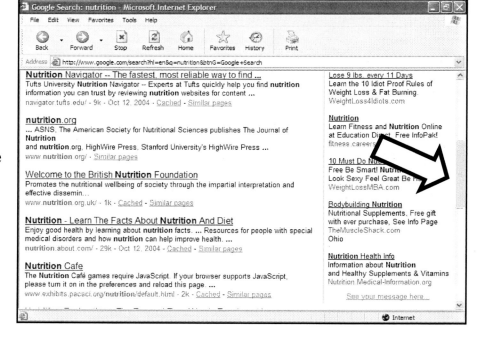

Step 2:
Click the NEXT
link.

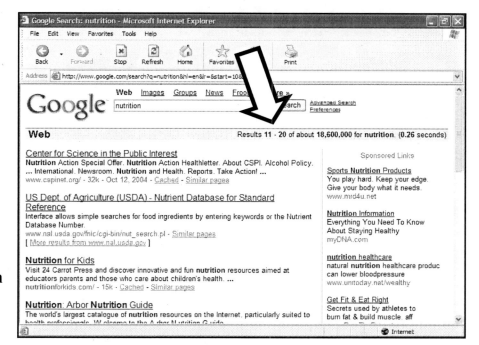

Search page 2
displaying
results eleven
thru twenty.

For Practice:
Open another
web page using
the links
provided.

Use the BACK
button to return
to this results
page.

Chapter 5: Search Engines!

Try a third time.

Scroll down to the bottom of the results page.

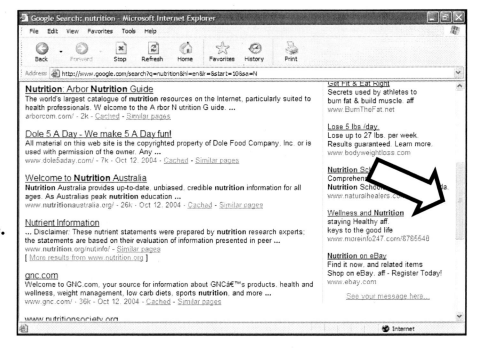

Click the NEXT link to move to the next page of search results.

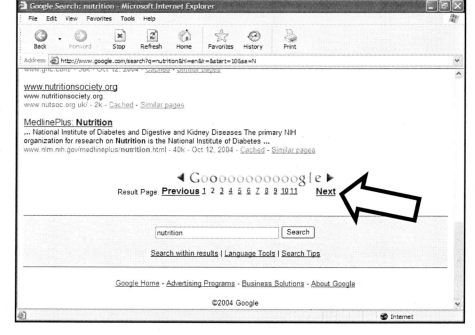

Chapter 5: Search Engines!

Filtering the Search Results

After looking through the first few pages of web page results, you might determine the topic you chose is too general/broad. The search engine allows you to add additional search terms (topics) to focus the search results. Adding search terms will shorten the results list and only display web pages which use all of your terms.

To add other search terms, find the search input box located at the very top or bottom of the results pages. The input box (white box) will contain the original search topic (nutrition). Click the left mouse button to activate the input box for typing. The blinking line (cursor) will appear at the end of the original search term "nutrition." Leave a space and then type in the next search term. Be sure to leave a space between each search term. For this example add the term "diabetes." When finished typing, either hit the enter key on the keyboard or click your mouse on the "Google Search" Button. The search engine will generate a new, more specific list of results using both the terms "nutrition" and "diabetes."

Filtering the Search Results: Step by Step Instructions

1. Find the search input box located at the very top or bottom of the results page.
2. Position the mouse pointer at the end of the input box and click the left mouse button to activate the input box.
3. Leave a space and then type in the next search term.
4. When finished typing, either hit the enter key on the keyboard or click your mouse on the SEARCH Button.

Chapter 5: Search Engines!

Filtering the Search Results: Visual Guide

Step 1:
Locate the search input box located at the very top or bottom of the results pages.

Step 2:
Position the mouse pointer at the end of the input box and click the left mouse button.

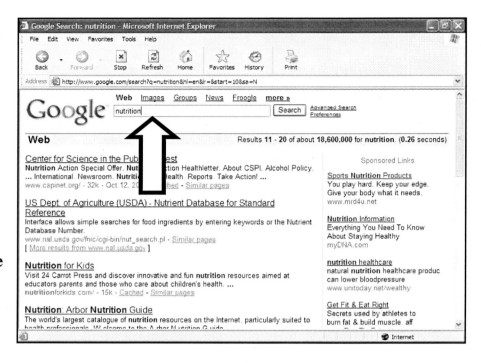

Step 3:
Put a space in and then type in the next search term.

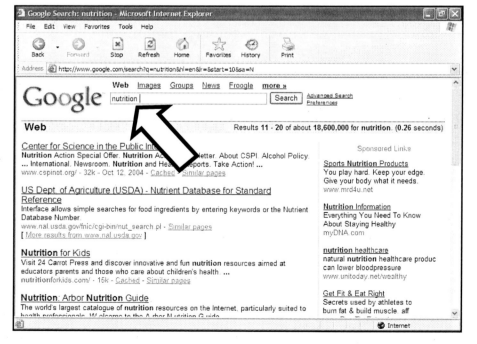

Step 4:
When finished typing, hit the enter key on the keyboard or click your mouse on the SEARCH button.

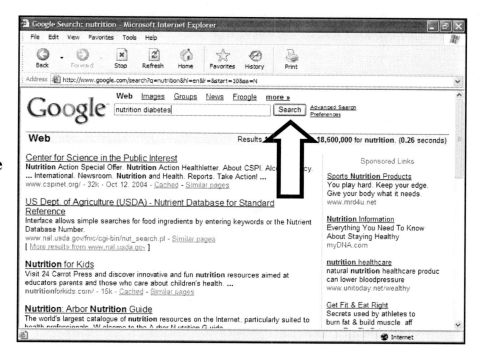

You will get a new Results Page.

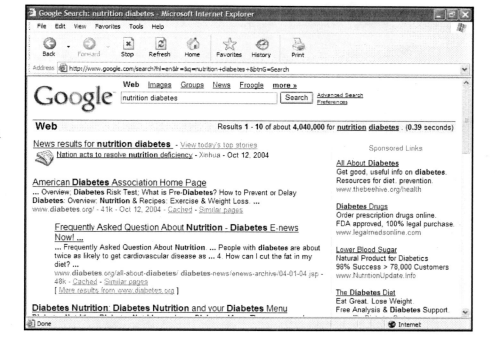

Look at the blue results line. Notice that when you added an additional search term, the results list decreased from approximately 18 million to just over 4 million web pages. After looking at a few more pages, add another search term and continue to focus the results list. For this example, add the term "recipes."

Step 1:
Find the search input box located at very bottom of the results pages by scrolling down the page.

Continue scrolling down the page.

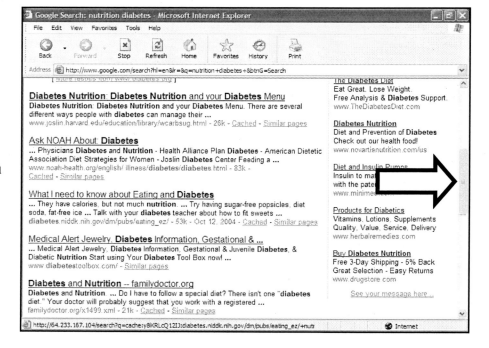

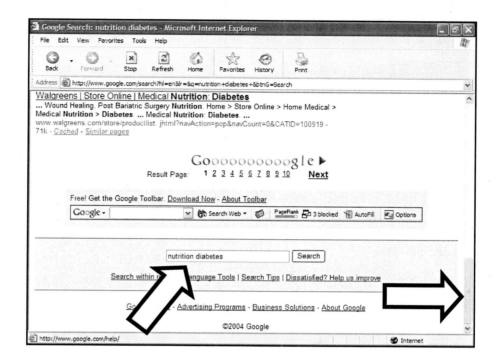

The Search Box.

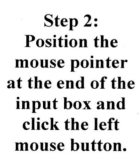

Step 2: Position the mouse pointer at the end of the input box and click the left mouse button.

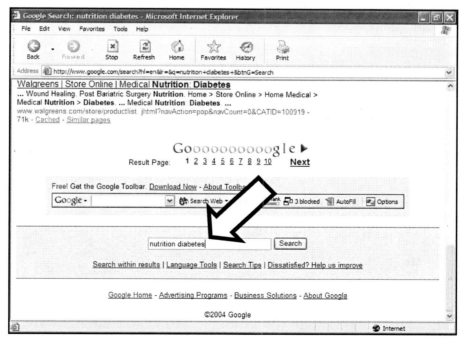

Step 3:
Put in a space and then type in the next search term.

Search term: "recipes"

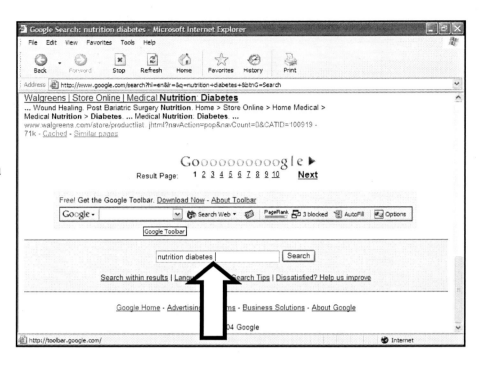

Step 4:
When finished typing, hit the Enter key on the keyboard or click your mouse on the SEARCH button.

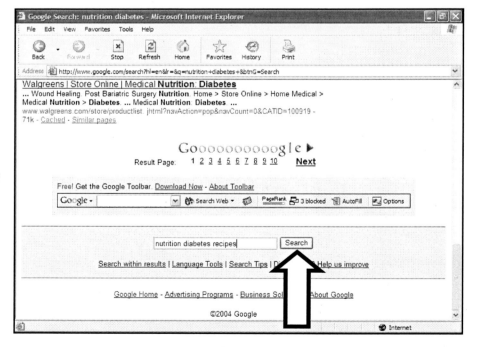

You will get a new Results Page.

 **QUESTION:** Can you start a search using multiple search terms?

ANSWER: Yes, multiple terms can be entered right from the start, but as a beginner it's best to start very generally. If the search is too focused, the information you are seeking might be filtered out. As you become more comfortable using the search engine, try searching using multiple terms.

Search for an Exact Name or Phrase

A Search Engine takes all the terms entered in the search input box and searches its database for each word individually. The search engine then compares the lists to locate web pages containing all of the search terms and displays the results.

A problem occurs when looking for a specific item using general search terms, e.g. John Smith. The search results may contain web pages with Louise Smith and John Jones, but not specifically "John Smith." To ensure the search results provide the right information, place exact names and phrases in quotation marks. The search engine will then look for web pages with the exact phrase, "John Smith."

Section 11: Using the Yahoo Search Engine

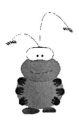

Google is not the only search engine available. There are many others, but you will notice that many of the search engines have features very similar to Google. An example of another search engine is Yahoo. Repeat the nutrition search, but use Yahoo instead of Google. Observe the similarities and differences between the Google and Yahoo main pages, as well as their search result pages. To get to Yahoo, conduct a specific search by typing its web address into your browser's address line. Yahoo's website address is www.yahoo.com.

Specific Search: Step by Step Instructions
1. **Obtain a website address for a search engine (ex: www.yahoo.com)**
2. **Position the mouse pointer over the input box located in the address line.**
3. **Click the left mouse button one time.**
4. **Press the backspace key or the delete key on the keyboard to erase the highlighted text.**
5. **Type the new website address in the input box: www.yahoo.com**
6. **Press the Enter Key on your keyboard to go to the website.**

Chapter 5: Search Engines!

Specific Search: Visual Guide

Step 1:
Obtain a
website address
www.yahoo.com

Step 2:
Position the
mouse pointer
over the input
box located in
the address line.

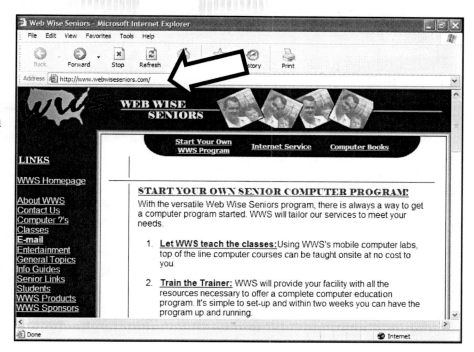

Step 3:
Click the left
mouse button
one time.

Step 4:
Press the
backspace key
or the delete key
on the keyboard
to erase the
highlighted text.

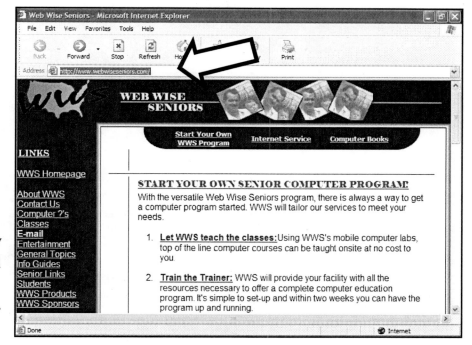

Step 5:
Type the new website address in the input box.

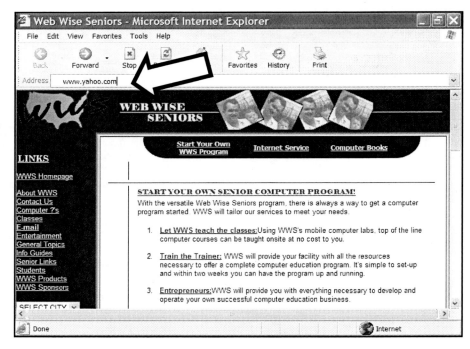

Step 6:
Press the Enter Key on your keyboard to go to the website.

Result of the specific search.

Chapter 5: Search Engines!

You have accomplished the first step in using a search engine. You opened the search engine website www.yahoo.com by completing a specific search using the website address and the browser address bar. The next objective is to use the search engine to search for information on the topic "nutrition."

Using a Search Engine: Step by Step Instructions

1. **Open the search engine website: (www.yahoo.com).**
2. **Type the search term(s) into the input box provided.**
3. **Press the Enter key on the keyboard or click the "YAHOO SEARCH" button located on the screen.**

Using a Search Engine: Visual Guide

Step 1:
Open the search engine website.

www.yahoo.com

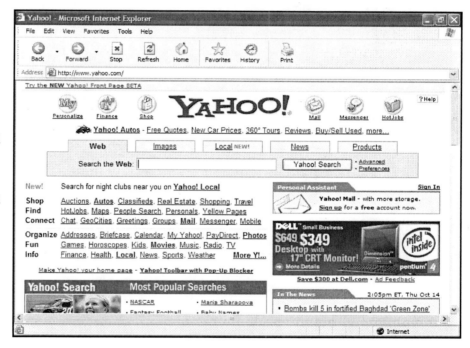

Chapter 5: Search Engines!

Step 2:
Type the search term(s) into the input box provided.

Step 3:
Press the Enter key on the keyboard or click the YAHOO SEARCH button located on the screen.

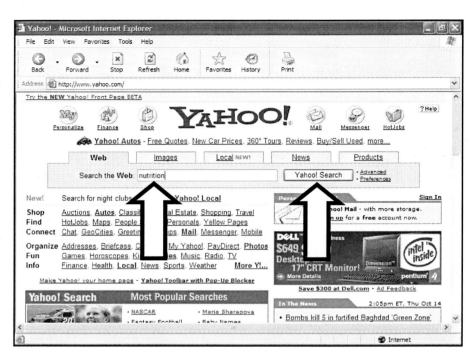

<u>RESULTS PAGE</u>

Search Input Box.

Blue Results Line.

Web Page List.

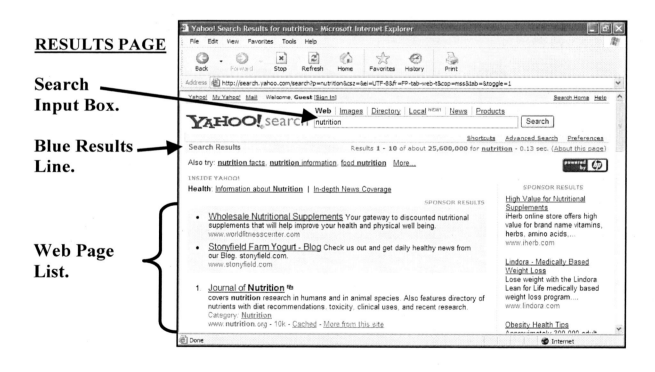

Below the blue line, the first ten websites will be listed. Each list will include a description, the web page address, and a link to the web page. The links are the blue underlined words. Move the mouse pointer over a link and the pointer will change from an arrow into a hand. Remember this is how the browser indicates a link. Click on the link. The web page will be displayed in the browser window. When you are done viewing the web page, click the back button until you return to the search results page.

Scroll down the screen using the window scroll bar to see the remainder of the results on the page. Near the bottom of the results page are numbers linking the first page, containing sites 1-10, to the second page containing sites 11-20, etc. Click the left mouse button on the number and the page will be displayed on the screen. There is also a "Next" link which you can use to move to the next ten results.

Practice opening web pages from the provided results list. When you want to return to the search list, click the Back button located on the browser toolbar. This will return you to the previous page. Move to the next page of results and open a few more pages.

Open a Web Page from the Results List:
Step by Step Instructions
1. **Move the mouse pointer over the link (blue underlined words).**
   - **The pointer will change from an arrow into a hand.**
2. **Click on the link using the left mouse button.**
   - **The web page will be displayed in the browser window.**

Chapter 5: Search Engines!

Open a Web Page from the Results List: Visual Guide

**Step 1:
Scroll down the
results page and
move the mouse
pointer over the
link.**

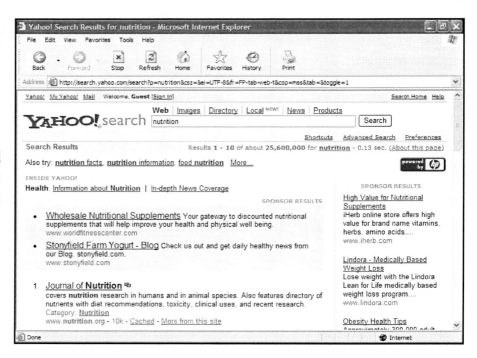

**Step 2:
Click on the
link using the
left mouse
button.**

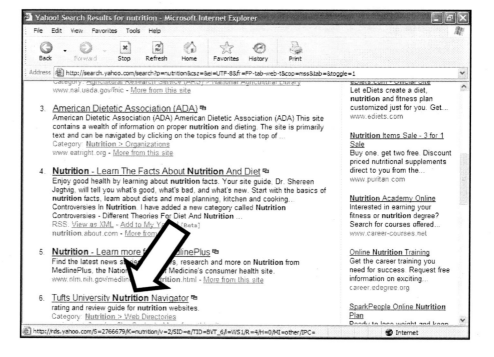

Step 3:
Click on an
internal web
page link using
the left mouse
button.

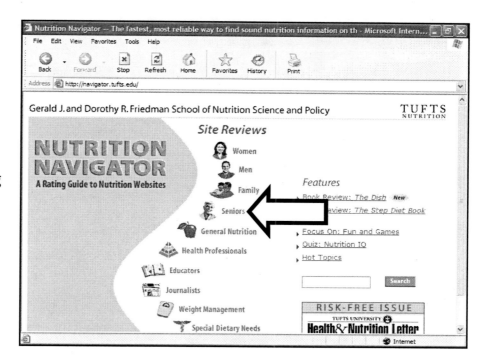

Step 4:
Return to the
Yahoo Search
Results List.

Click the BACK
button.

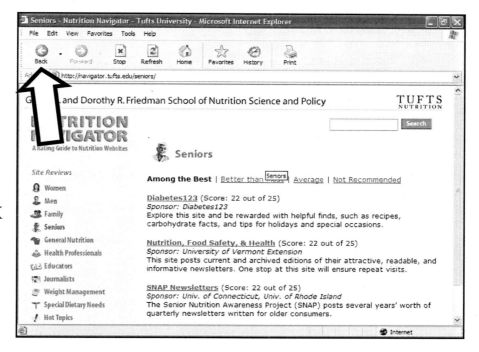

Continue Step 4:
Return to the Yahoo Search Results List by clicking the BACK button.

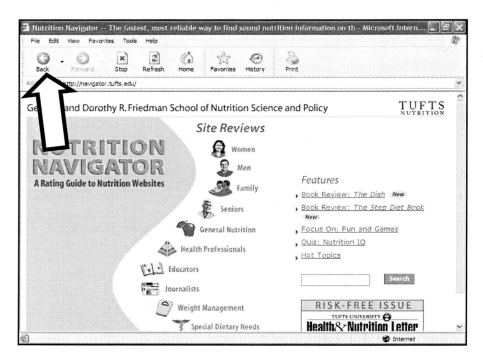

Step 5:
Scroll down the results page to open the second page of results.

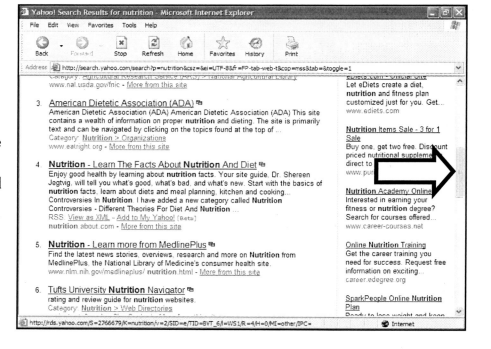

Step 6:
Click NEXT to move to the next page of search results.

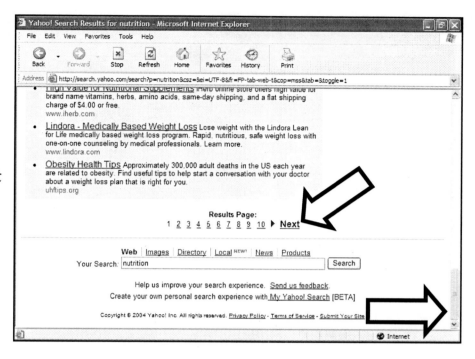

Search Results Page 2.

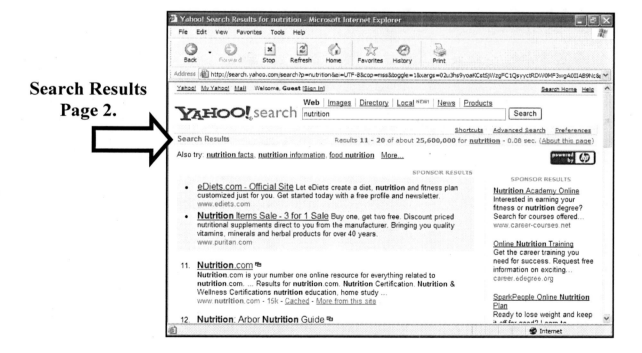

For practice, open a few additional web pages from the results list.

Section 12: "Page Cannot be Found" Error Message

"Page Cannot be Found Error"

If you are searching through the Internet and a "Page Cannot Be Found" screen pops up, do not worry. The "Page Cannot Be Found" screen appears under many circumstances. Some common reasons include: the web page was removed from the website, the address of the web page has changed, the web site is <u>temporarily</u> not working, or the web address was typed incorrectly. As the Internet gets larger, it is harder for the browser to keep track of all of the pages and websites, resulting in more frequent "Page Cannot Be Found" errors.

If you experience a "Page Cannot Be Found" error screen, just click the Back button in the browser toolbar to return to the previous page. You may want to try to access the site later since the error may have been caused by a temporary Internet glitch. If the error occurred after you attempted a specific search, check the address you typed in the address line. Make certain the address is typed and spelled correctly. If all else fails, try to locate another website which can provide you with the information you were seeking.

Chapter 5: Search Engines!

Page cannot be found screen.

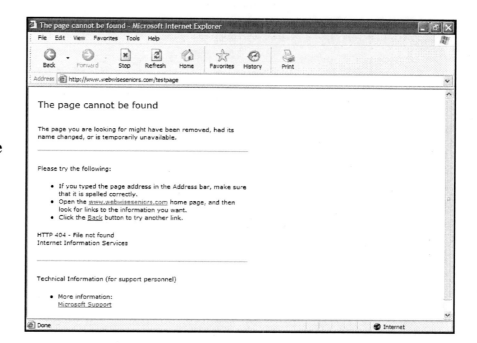

Chapter 5: Search Engines!

Chapter 6

Favorites List!

What You Will Learn in this Chapter
✓ What is the Favorites list?
✓ How do you add a website to the Favorites list?
✓ How do you open a web page from the Favorites list?
✓ How do you organize the Favorites list?

Section 13: Using the Favorites List

Favorites/Bookmarks

Internet browsers have the capability to store and remember website addresses. Website addresses are saved in a list commonly referred to as the Favorites list or bookmark list. Saving a website address is called "adding a favorite" or "bookmarking" a page. You no longer have to remember a website's address; just save it to your Favorites list.

Add a Website to the Favorites List

In order to add a website to your Favorites list, first open the web page in your browser. For example, open the Web Wise Seniors website (www.webwiseseniors.com). Once the page is open, click the Favorites button (star) located in the browser toolbar. The browser window will split into two sections. The left section displays the Favorites list, while the right section displays the web page. Using the mouse, click the "Add" button, found in the upper left-hand corner of the Favorites list. A message box will appear. The title of the current web page will be displayed in the name input box. If you want to store the website address under its current name, simply click on the OK button. To change the name, position the mouse pointer after the web page title located in the white input box. Click the left mouse button. The blinking cursor will appear in the input box. Erase everything in the input box by using the backspace key on the keyboard. Choose a name and type it into the box. Click the OK button when finished. The new website will be added to your Favorites list.

When you are finished adding the new website, close the Favorites list by clicking on the Favorites button in the browser toolbar. The left column will close. The web page will be fully displayed in the window. The Favorites button acts like an open/close switch and will open and close the left section of the browser screen containing the Favorite list.

Add a Website to the Favorites List: Step by Step Instructions
1. Open the web page you want to add in the browser.
2. Click the FAVORITES button located in the browser toolbar.
3. Click the ADD button.
4. Check the Name Bar to make sure the website name is correct.
5. Click the OK button.

Add a Website to the Favorites List: Visual Guide

Step 1:
Open the web
page in the
browser.

Step 2:
Click the
FAVORITES
button located
in the browser
toolbar.

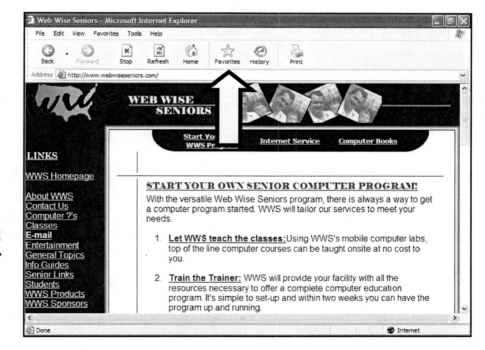

Chapter 6: Favorites List!

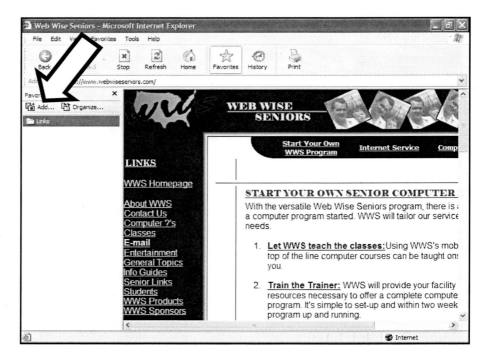

Step 3:
Click the ADD button.

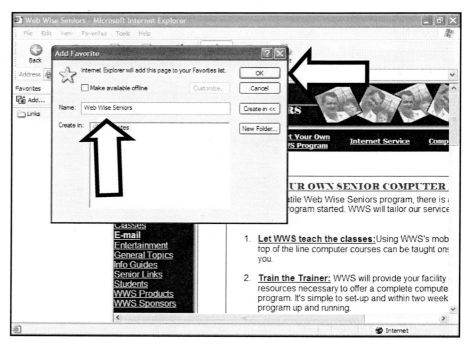

Step 4:
Check the Name Box to make sure the website name is correct.

Step 5:
Click the OK button.

Chapter 6: Favorites List!

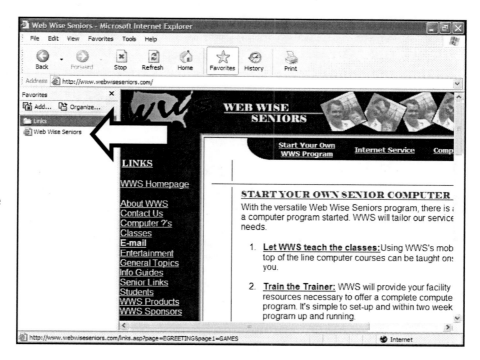

The new item will be displayed in the Favorites list.

For practice add some additional sites to the Favorites list. Do a specific search for each of the following websites and add them to your Favorites list.

www.google.com   www.yahoo.com   www.mapquest.com

www.expedia.com   www.travelocity.com   www.aaa.com

Using the Favorites List

The Favorites list can be used to go directly to any website saved to the list. Open your Favorites list by clicking on the Favorites button located in the browser toolbar. The browser window splits into two sections. The left section displays the Favorites list. Choose the name of the website you want to go to and click on it. The browser will automatically open that web page. Using your newly created Favorites, click the listing for Google. Notice how the browser opens the page. Now, select Web Wise Seniors. If you want to have the web page fill your window, close the Favorites list by clicking on the Favorites button in the browser toolbar.

The Favorites list can also be accessed via the Favorites menu located at the top of the browser window. Click on the Favorites menu and the Favorites list will appear. Click on the desired listing and that web page will be displayed. The menu provides the same options as the toolbar button. Just like everything else in computers, there are multiple ways to accomplish the same task.

Chapter 6: Favorites List!

Open a Favorite: Step by Step Instructions

1. Click the FAVORITES button located in the browser toolbar.
2. Once the list opens, click on your desired listing.
3. To close the Favorites list, click the FAVORITES button located in the browser toolbar.

Open a Favorite: Visual Guide

**Step 1:
Click the
FAVORITES
button located
in the browser
toolbar.**

Chapter 6: Favorites List!

Step 2:
Choose the desired listing with your mouse and click on it.

Step 3:
Click the FAVORITES button located in the browser toolbar to close the Favorites list.

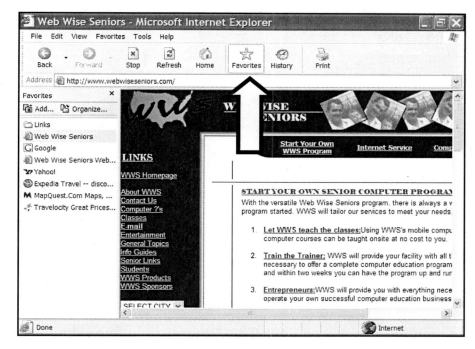

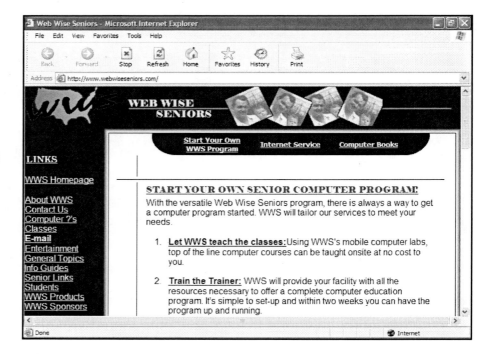

The website is displayed in your browser window.

Section 14: Organizing the Favorites List

Organizing the Favorites

Over time, the Favorites list can become extensive and unorganized. Keep the Favorites list easy-to-use by organizing it. You can rename favorites, delete favorites, or create folders to group common listings.

The first step in the organization process is to open the Favorites list by clicking the Favorites button (star) located in the browser toolbar. The browser window will split into two sections. The left section will display the Favorites list. Using the mouse, click the "Organize" button located just above the Favorites list in the left section of the window. The organize window will appear. The organize window allows you to rename, delete, move, and create folders. Creating folders enables you to organize the list by topic.

Earlier, you added multiple travel websites to your Favorites list. By creating a "Travel Sites" folder, you can keep all of these Favorites together. Click the Create Folder button located in the Organize Favorites window. A new folder will appear in the list with the name "New Folder" highlighted in blue. The computer is ready for you to rename the folder. Type the words "Travel Sites." The words in blue (New Folder) will disappear and will be replaced by your typing (Travel Sites). When you are finished, press the Enter key on the keyboard to accept the name.

Now you need to place your travel websites into your new folder. To place a favorite inside the new folder, click the name of the desired favorite. The names of the websites are found in the box to the right of the organize window. Click the "Move to Folder" button. A "Browse for Folder" window will appear. The "Browse for Folder" window provides a list of your Favorite folders. Click on the name of the folder into which you are moving your favorite. The folder name will turn blue. Click the OK button. The "Browse for Folder" window will close and the favorite will be placed inside the selected folder. To move another favorite: first click the favorite, second click the Move to Folder button, third select the folder, and fourth click the OK button. When you are finished organizing the Favorites, click the Close button in the bottom right corner of the "Organize Favorites" window.

Organize the Favorites List: Step by Step Instructions
1. **Click the FAVORITES button located in the browser toolbar.**
2. **Click the ORGANIZE button located above the Favorites list.**
3. **Click the CREATE FOLDER button.**
4. **Type in the folder's name.**
5. **Press the Enter key on the keyboard.**
   - **The new folder has been created and will be displayed in the Favorites list.**
6. **To move a favorite into a folder, click once on the website name.**
7. **Click the MOVE TO FOLDER button.**
8. **Click once on the folder's name from the list provided.**
9. **Click the OK button.**
10. **Repeat steps 5 thru 8 to move additional list items.**
11. **Click the CLOSE button.**

Chapter 6: Favorites List!

Organize the Favorites List: Visual Guide

Step 1:
Click the
FAVORITES
button located
in the browser
toolbar.

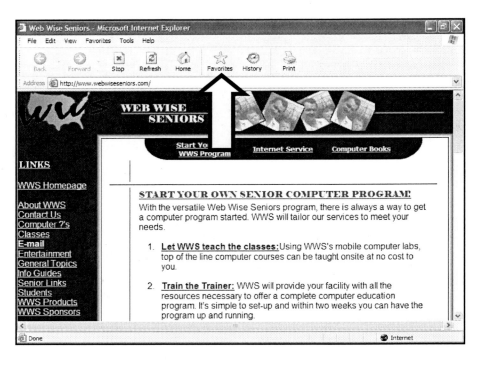

Step 2:
Click the
ORGANIZE
button located
above the list of
Favorites.

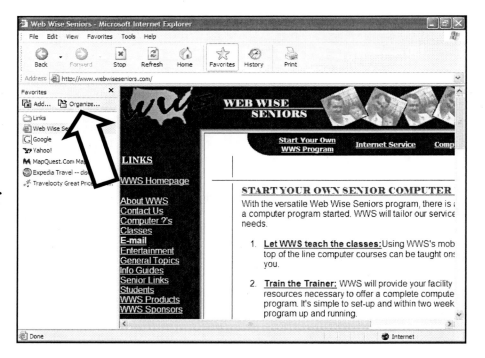

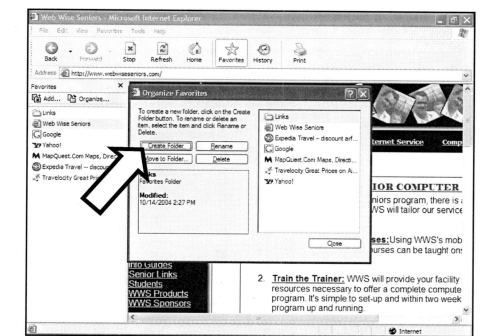

Step 3:
Click the
CREATE
FOLDER
button.

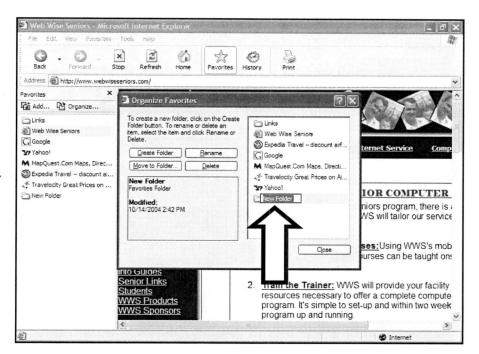

Step 4:
Type in the
name of the new
folder.

Step 5:
Press the Enter key on the keyboard.

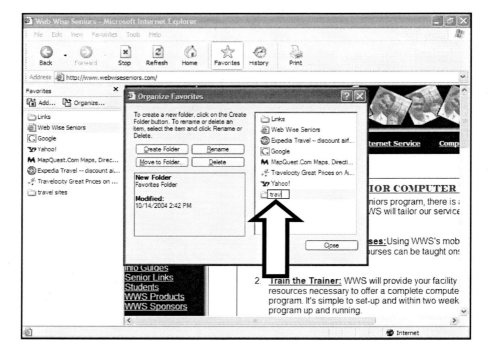

Newly Created Folder.

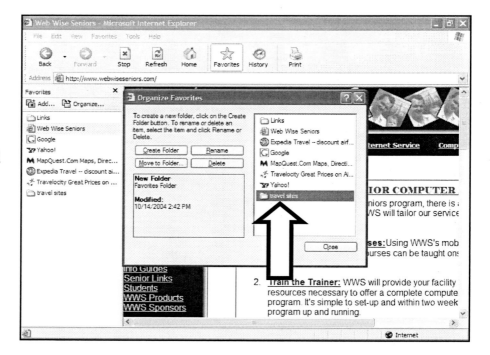

Step 6:
Click once on the name of the website you want to move into the new folder.

Step 7:
Click the MOVE TO FOLDER button.

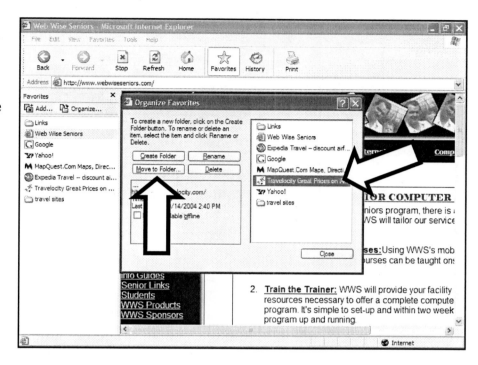

Step 8:
Click once on the folder's name from the list provided.

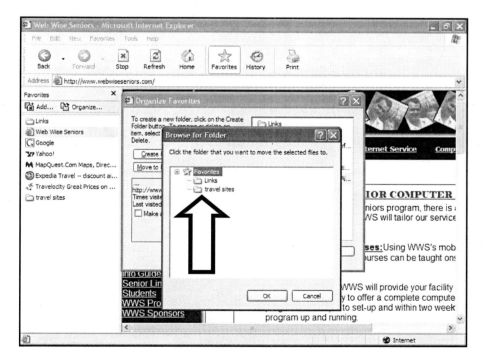

**Step 9:
Click the OK
button.**

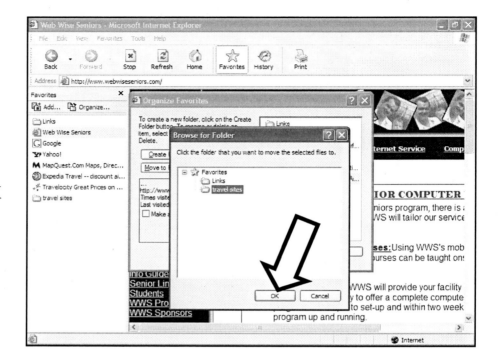

**Step 10:
Repeat steps 5
thru 8 to move
additional list
items.**

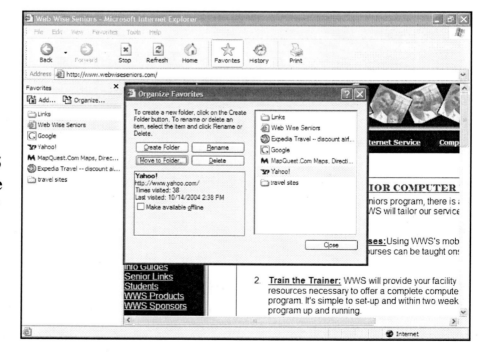

**Step 11:
Click the
CLOSE button.**

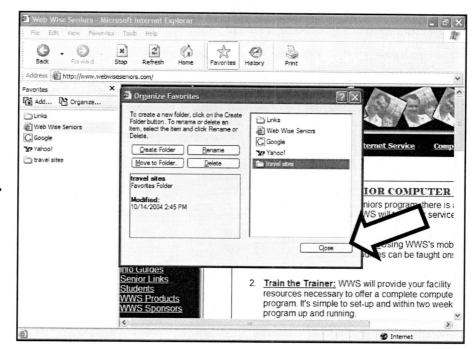

**The Newly
Organized
Favorites List.**

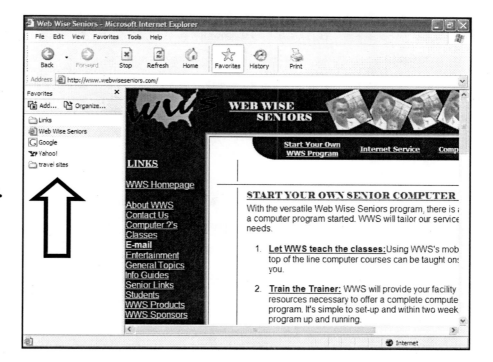

Chapter 6: Favorites List!

Opening a Favorite Located in a Favorites List Folder

Selecting a favorite from a folder is very similar to opening a normal favorite. Once the Favorites list is visible, click on the desired folder. The browser will display the Favorite in the folder underneath the folder's name. Click on the desired favorite. The browser will open the page. To display the website using the entire browser window, close the Favorites list by clicking on the Favorites button in the browser toolbar. Practice opening the sites listed in the "Travel Sites" folder.

Opening a Favorite Located in a Folder: Step by Step Instructions

1. **Click once on the folder's name to display the Favorites in the folder.**
2. **Click the desired favorite from the list provided.**
3. **Click the FAVORITES button, located in the browser toolbar, to close the Favorites list.**

Opening a Favorite Located in a Folder: Visual Guide

Step 1: Click once on the folder's name to display the Favorites in the folder.

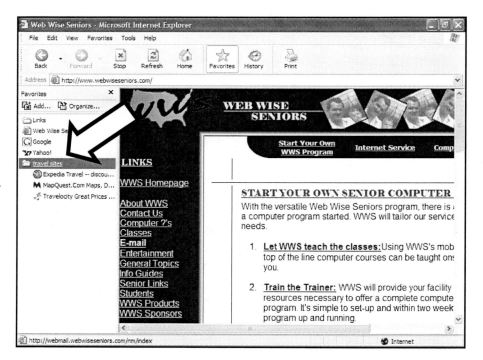

Chapter 6: Favorites List!

Step 2:
Click the desired favorite from the list provided.

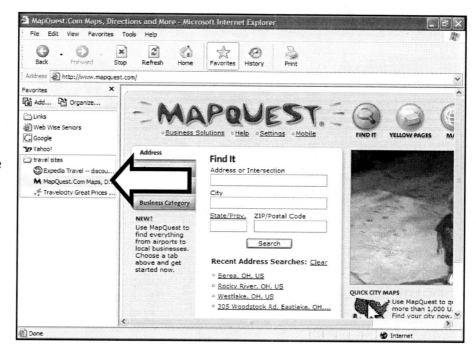

Step 3:
Click the FAVORITES button, located in the browser toolbar, to close the Favorites list.

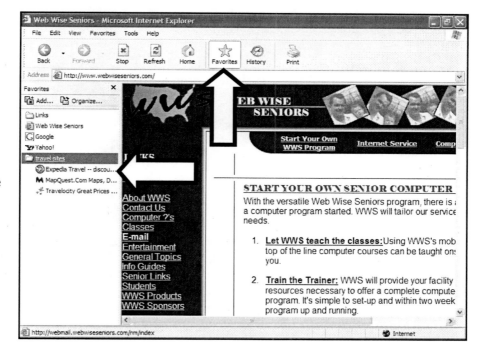

Full-size browser window.

For Practice: Click another favorite from the list provided.

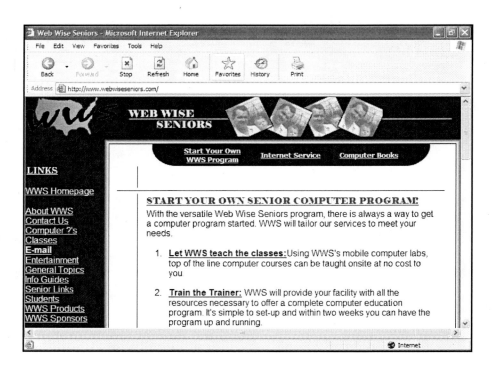

Chapter 7

History List!

What You Will Learn in this Chapter
✓ What is the History list?
✓ How do you use the History list?
✓ How do you erase the History list?

Section 15: Using the History List

Your browser is designed to keep track of the websites you have visited while on the Internet. This is called the History. Why would a History be beneficial to a computer user? Well, the History list enables the computer to show you the links you have opened in the past. It also helps you easily return to websites you've viewed recently.

The History list displays the name of each website you have viewed. It keeps this list for approximately 20 days. The list is separated by days and weeks. So, if you were on the Internet on Monday, the computer will have a list of all the websites you visited on Monday. Under the name of the day, each website has a folder containing links to the website pages you visited. To open the folder and view the page links, click the left mouse button on the website name. A list of web pages will appear indented below the folder name. To look at a desired web page, put the mouse pointer over the name of the web page. The pointer will turn into a hand. When you click the left mouse button, the computer will go to that page. Remember, the browser is typically set to record your Internet travel for 20 days. After 20 days have passed, the oldest items will automatically be erased to make room for newly visited sites.

Links you have opened change color. Typically, unvisited links are blue while recently visited links are purple. This enables you to quickly identify the website links you have already seen, saving you the time and effort of repeatedly opening the same websites.

You can also use the History list to see the websites your computer has been to when other people have used it. For example, you can use the History list to find out what websites your grandson went to while he was visiting or what your spouse is buying (on the Internet) for your birthday. We are not suggesting you spy on others, but the option is available if you need it.   But, remember, if you can spy on someone in your household, someone in your household can spy on you.

Opening the History List

Open the History list by clicking your mouse on the History button in the browser toolbar. The button may or may not be named History, but it is usually represented by an image of a clock or sundial. The browser screen will split into two sections when the History list is opened. The left section displays the History list, while the right section displays the current website.

Using the History Button: Step by Step Instructions

1. Click the HISTORY button located in the browser toolbar.
2. Click the day or week you want to view.
3. Click the website name to display a detailed list of the web pages visited.
4. Click the web page name to open the page in the browser window.
5. Click the HISTORY button located in the browser toolbar to close the list.

Using the History Button: Visual Guide

Step 1:
Click the HISTORY button located in the browser toolbar.

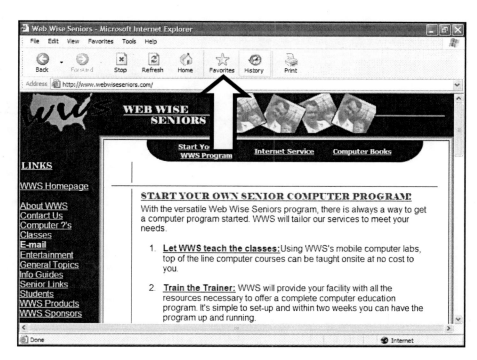

Step 2:
Click on the day or week you want to review.

Step 3:
Click the website name to display a detailed list of web pages visited on that particular website.

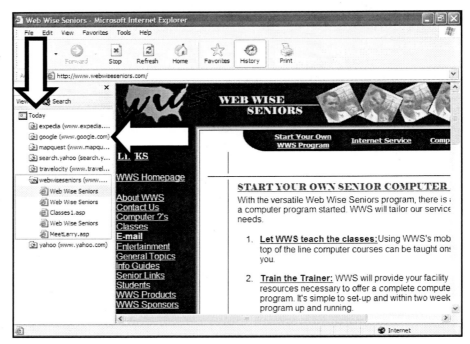

Step 4:
Click the web page name to open the page in the browser window.

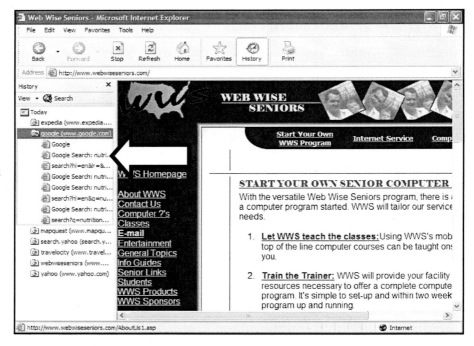

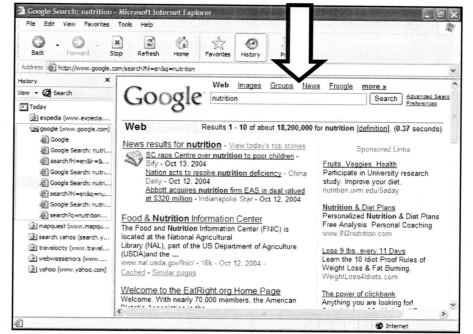

The web page is now open in the window on the right side.

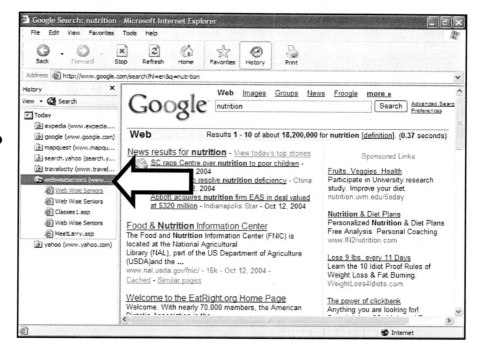

Practice

Step 3: Click the website name to display a detailed list of web pages visited on that particular website.

Practice

**Step 4:
Click the web
page name to
open the page in
the browser
window.**

**The web page is
now open in the
window on the
right side.**

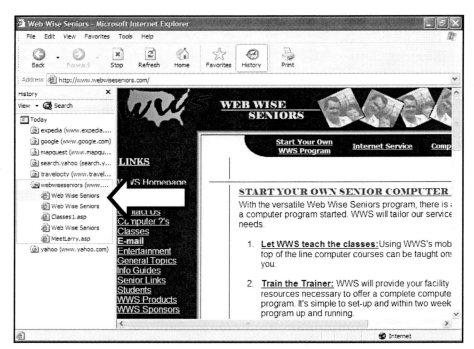

Practice

**Step 5:
Click the
HISTORY
button located
in the browser
toolbar.**

**The History List
is now closed.**

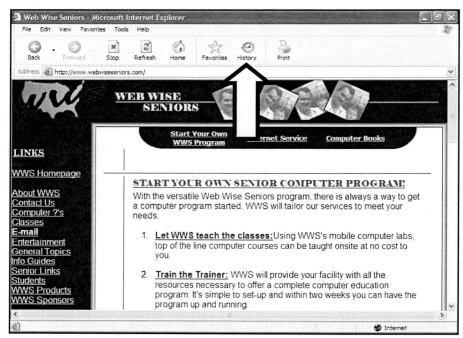

Section 16: Erasing the History List

Erasing the History List

There may be times you wish to erase the History list. Let's say you were buying a gift for someone over the Internet and you did not want to risk them finding out. Erasing the History list ensures someone cannot discover where you have gone on the Internet.

To erase the History list, first locate the Tools menu just below the browser window title bar. Click once on the heading Tools to open the menu. Move the mouse pointer down the menu list and position it over the last selection, "Internet Options." It will turn blue. Clicking the left mouse button opens the Internet Options window. The window is divided into three sections. If you look in the last (third) part of the window, entitled History, you will find the History list controls. To erase the History, find the "Clear History" button and click it with the mouse. A message box appears asking if you are sure you want to erase your computer's History. Click the Yes button. Click the OK button located on the bottom of the Internet Options window to close the window. To make sure the list was erased, open the History and check.

Erasing the History List: Step by Step Instructions
1. **Click the TOOLS menu.**
2. **Click INTERNET OPTIONS.**
3. **Find the History option in the lower third portion of the window.**
4. **Click the CLEAR HISTORY button.**
5. **Click the YES button on the message window.**
6. **Click the OK button.**

Chapter 7: History List!

Erasing the History List: Visual Guide

**Step 1:
Click the
TOOLS menu.**

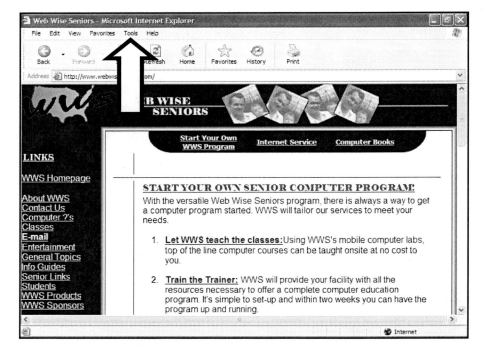

**Step 2:
Click
INTERNET
OPTIONS.**

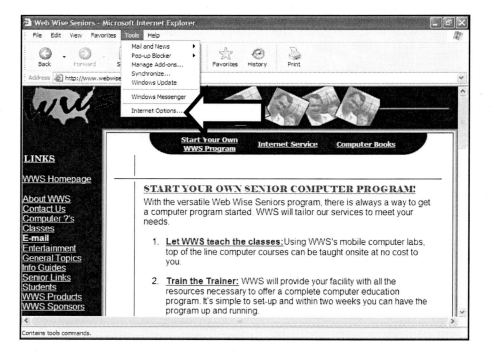

Step 3:
Find the History option in the lower third portion of the window.

Step 4:
Click the CLEAR HISTORY button.

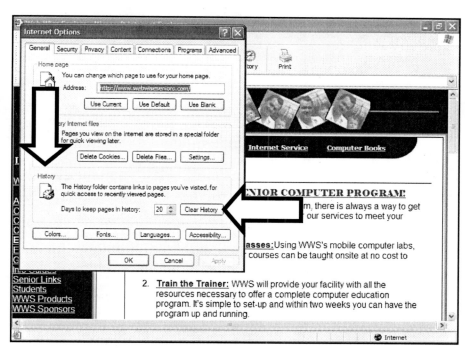

Step 5:
Click the YES button on the message window.

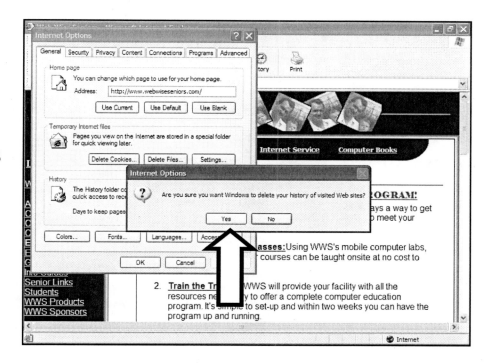

Chapter 7: History List!

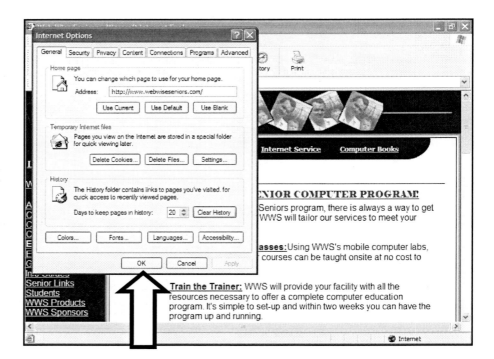

**Step 5:
Click the OK
button.**

Now, verify that the history list was erased.

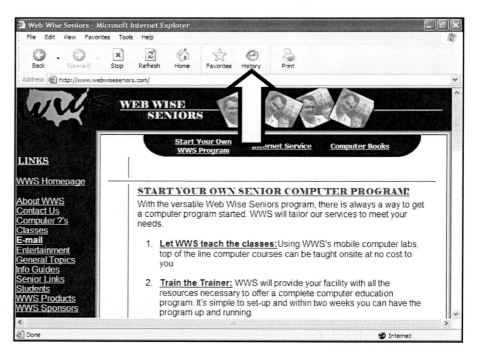

**Step 1:
Click the
HISTORY
button located
in the browser
toolbar.**

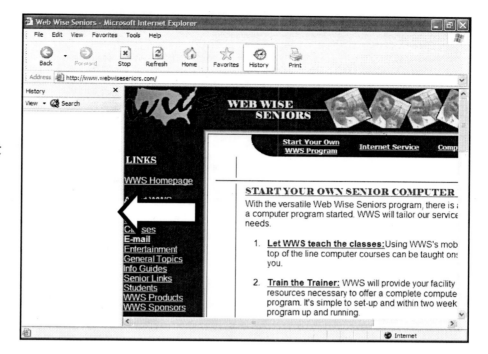

The history list is empty.

Step 2: Click the HISTORY button located in the browser toolbar to close the list.

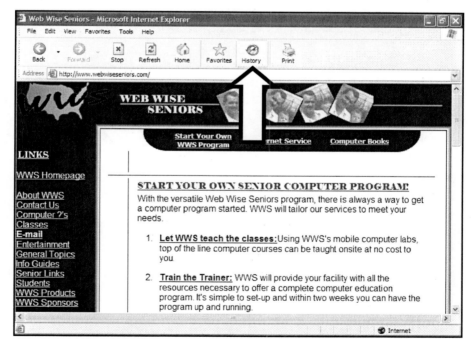

Chapter 7: History List!

Chapter 8

Changing the Home Page!

What You Will Learn in this Chapter
✓ What is a Home Page?
✓ How do you change the browser Home Page?

Section 17: Browser Home Page

Once you have connected to the Internet and have opened your browser, most browsers automatically display a web page. This starting page is called the Home Page. Internet Service Providers, during setup, typically set your computer to open to their main web page. If your friend has a different ISP, your starting page (Home Page) will be different from your friend's Home Page.

As you become familiar with different websites, you may decide to change your Home Page. You can set your Home Page to any site you like. Often a person will set the Home Page to a site that provides one of the following services: news, weather, search engine, e-mail, or a site providing useful resources.

To set the Home Page, find Tools menu located just below the browser's title bar. Click once on the Tools menu to open it. Move the mouse pointer down the menu list and position it over the last selection, Internet Options, which will turn blue. Click the left mouse button to open the Internet Options window. Located at the top of the window is the heading Home Page.

There are four ways to set your the Home Page. If you know the web address of the website you want as your Home Page, type the address in the input box provided. Another option is to have your browser open to the web page you want as your Home Page, and click the "Use Current" button. The web page open in your browser will be set as your Home Page. A third option is to click the "Use Default" button. The computer manufacturer's website will be set as the Home Page. Finally, if you do like any of the above options, you can click the "Use Blank" button. The browser will always begin with a blank Home

Chapter 8: Changing the Home Page!

Page. Once you have changed your Home Page, click the OK button to close the Internet Options window.

If you change the browser's Home Page, the Home button located on the browser toolbar will also be affected. No matter where you are on the Internet, clicking the Home button in the toolbar will take you directly to the website you set as your browser's Home Page.

Changing the Home Page: Step by Step Instructions
1. **Click the TOOLS menu.**
2. **Click INTERNET OPTIONS.**
3. **Type the new website address into the input box provided.**
4. **Click the OK button.**

Changing the Home Page: Visual Guide

Step 1:
Click the
TOOLS menu.

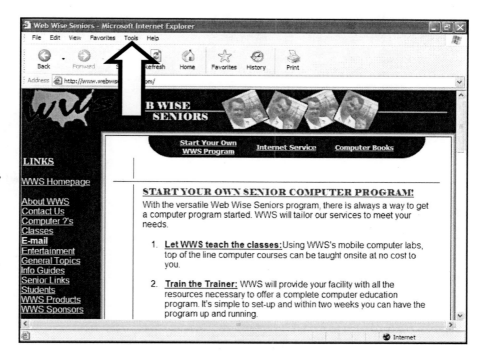

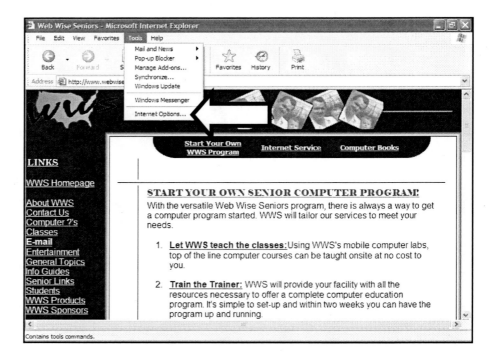

**Step 2:
Click
INTERNET
OPTIONS.**

**Step 3:
Type in the
website address
in the input box
provided.**

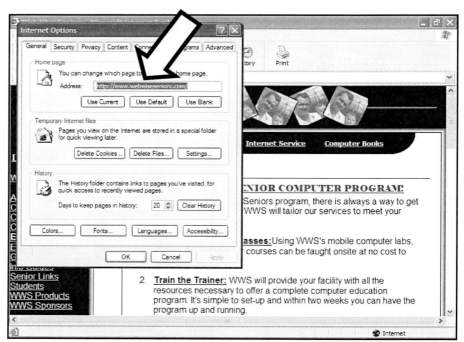

Chapter 8: Changing the Home Page!

**Step 4:
Click the OK
button.**

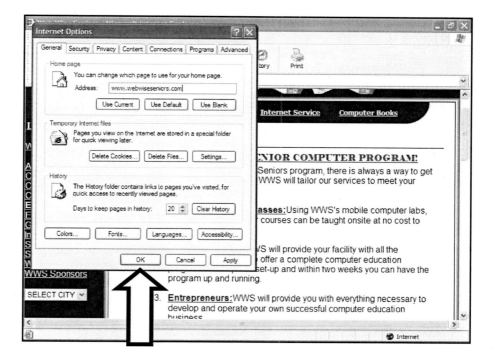

***Test the Home
Page:***

**Click the
HOME button
located in the
browser
toolbar.**

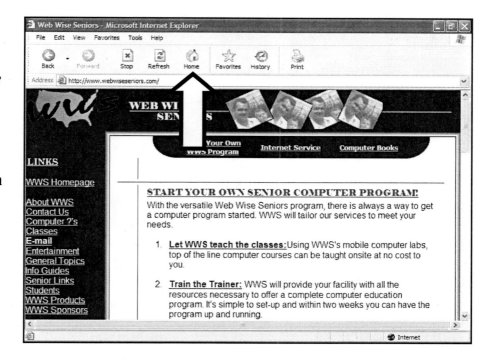

Chapter 8: Changing the Home Page!

Chapter 9

Downloading & Installation!

What You Will Learn in this Chapter

✓ What is downloading?
✓ What can you download from the Internet?
✓ How to download from the Internet.
✓ What is installation?
✓ How to install a new program.
✓ How to open a newly installed program.
✓ How to download and install Adobe® Reader and RealPlayer®.

Section 18: Downloading from the Internet

Every once in a while, when you are on the Internet, you find a program, picture, song, etc. that you want to permanently have on your computer. Taking something from the Internet and placing in on your computer is called Downloading. Music, pictures, programs, and videos are just a few of the items people download. The download process is similar to going to a website and clicking on a link. Instead of the link taking you to another web page, it opens a window prompting you to open or save the item (file) you want to download.

The first step in the downloading process is to find the item you wish to download. People often become aware of downloadable items via TV, magazines, radio, e-mail, or by word of mouth. In order to find the item, you may want to look at the website of the company which created the program/item. Locate the desired item. Most websites which have downloads available will provide instructions for downloading. (Links saying "Get It Now" or "Download Now" may be found next to the item you wish to download.) After you have clicked the link to start the download, a window will appear prompting you to open or save the file. Select the OPEN option to temporarily view the file from its original location. If you want to permanently keep the item, select SAVE to copy the item onto your computer. When downloading, most people use the save option.

If you choose save, the computer will open the Save window. From this point, the download process is identical to saving a document in a word processing program like Word. There are three steps in the process. First, you must tell the computer where you want to save the file. Second, you have to give the file a name. Third, you must click the Save button.

The first step is to tell the computer where you want to save the file. At the top of the save screen, is the heading SAVE IN: followed by a white box and a gray arrow pointing down. This gray arrow is called a drop down arrow. It tells the computer user that there are more options offered within the input box.

Chapter 9: Downloading & Installation!

When you click the gray arrow, a list will appear displaying the locations to which you can save your file. This box should say "Desktop." If it does not, you need to click on the drop down arrow and choose "Desktop" from the list. Once you have opened the list, place your mouse pointer over the option DESKTOP. It will turn blue. To make the selection, click the left mouse button. The drop down list will close and "Desktop" will be displayed in the "Save In" box.

The second step is to choose a name for the file. Located near the bottom of the save screen, you will see the heading "File Name:." To the right of the heading File Name: is a white input box containing the name of the file to be downloaded. The name in the input box is the website's suggestion for a name. If the suggestion looks good, move on to the third step in the save process.

The final step in the save process is to click the "Save" button. This button is located on the bottom right side of the save screen. When you click the "Save" button, the computer will close the save screen. The file will begin transferring (downloading) and saving it to your computer's main memory. A progress bar will appear on your screen showing the transfer. The window will tell you when the transfer is complete. After the file is completely downloaded, click the "Close" button on the progress window.

The download process is complete. Now, you need to locate the file on the computer and open it. Since you saved the file to the Desktop, that is where the downloaded program will appear. Minimize your browser window and look at the desktop. You will see a new icon (picture) representing the file. Double click the icon to open the file. If the downloaded file is music or video, the computer will automatically play the item. If the downloaded file is a letter or document, the computer will open the item in your word processing program.

If the downloaded file is a program, double clicking on the icon automatically starts the installation process. The installation process instructs the computer how to set up and use the new program. An installation window will appear and walk you through the setup steps. We will be discussing Installing in detail later in the chapter. Once the downloaded file is installed, you can open the program using the Start menu.

Downloading is similar to ordering from a catalog. First, you find the desired item in the catalog and call the company to place the order. The company then ships the item to you. After the mail carrier delivers the package, you open it to view the item. Depending on what you order, the item might need to be assembled before use. Assembling an item can be compared to installing a downloaded program.

Adobe® Acrobat Reader

We will download the program "Adobe Reader," also known as "Adobe Acrobat Reader," as an example of downloading. Adobe Reader is a free program available to anyone on the Internet. Basically, Adobe Reader is a program which allows people to read and print complicated documents (called .pdf files.) You will often see applications and tax forms in this format. To open the website, do a specific search using the website address www.adobe.com.

Downloading a Program from the Internet:
Step by Step Instructions

1. Find the program on the Internet that you would like to add to your computer.
2. Click the link that is similar to DOWNLOAD or GET IT NOW.
3. Choose the option SAVE.
4. Tell the computer where you would like to save the program.
   - Click the drop down arrow at the end of the "Save In:" box to choose a location.
   - NOTE: Make certain you remember the file name and the location where the computer is saving the program.
5. Click the SAVE button.
   - A progress bar will appear showing you how the download process is going.
   - The computer will notify you when the downloading process is complete.
6. Once your download is complete, click the CLOSE button located in the download progress window.
7. Click the MINIMIZE button (-) to hide the Internet browser window.

Chapter 9: Downloading & Installation!

Downloading a Program from the Internet: Visual Guide

Open the Adobe website.
www.adobe.com

Step 1:
Find the program on the Internet that you would like to download to your computer.

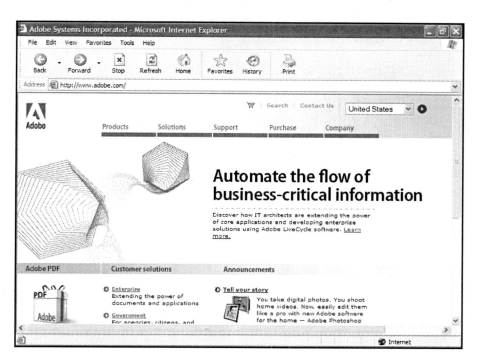

Click the Products link to display the list of available programs.

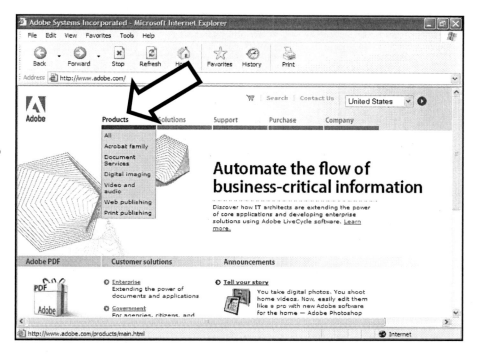

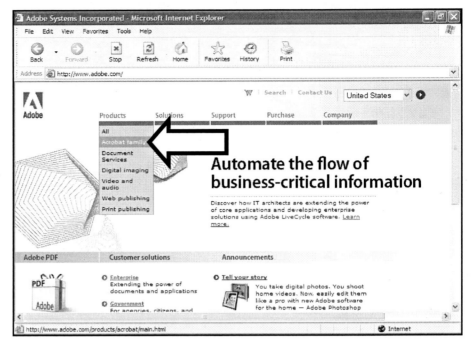

Click the Acrobat Family link displayed in the products list.

Locate the link to the Adobe Acrobat Reader program.

Hint: Scroll down. It is near the bottom of the web page.

Chapter 9: Downloading & Installation!

Click on the GET ADOBE READER link.

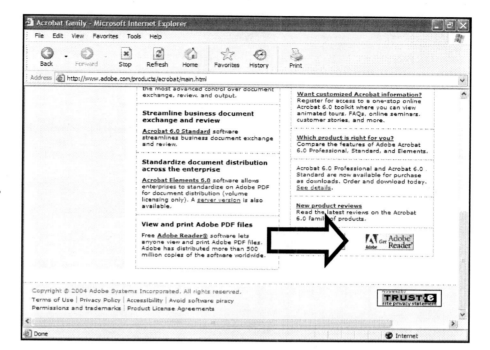

Read the program description. Click on the link FREE ADOBE READER.

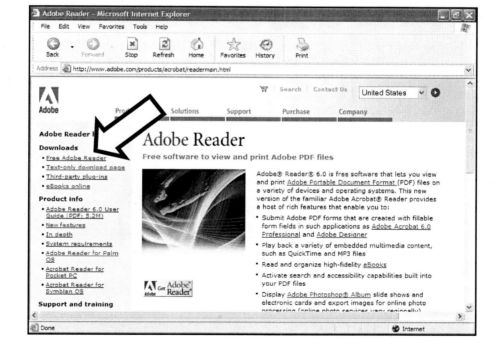

Read the download instructions and follow the instructions.

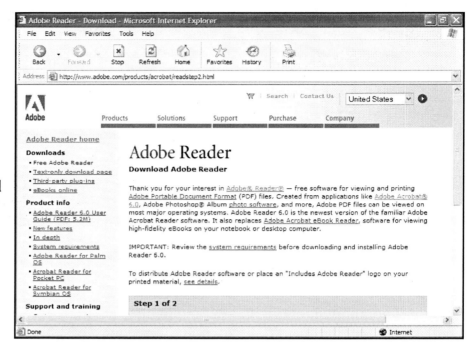

From the drop-down lists provided, choose your language *"English,"* platform *"Windows XP,"* and your Internet connection speed.

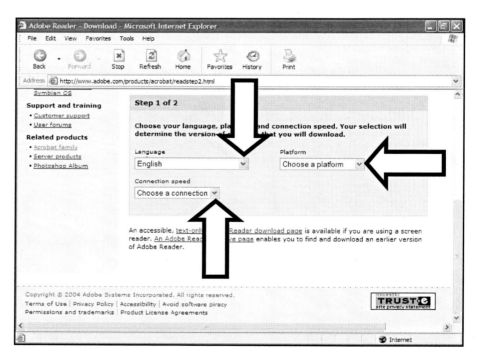

Click inside the little box indicating "Download the full version." A check mark should appear in the box.

Continue to scroll down the page.

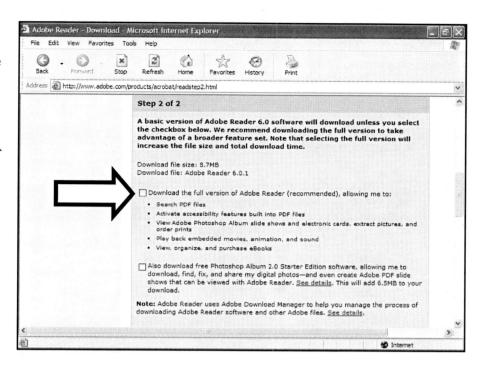

Scroll down the page to finish reading the download instructions.

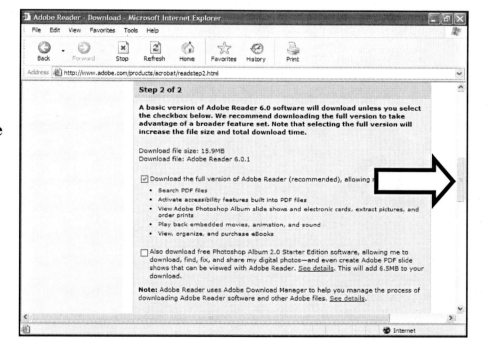

Click the CONTINUE button.

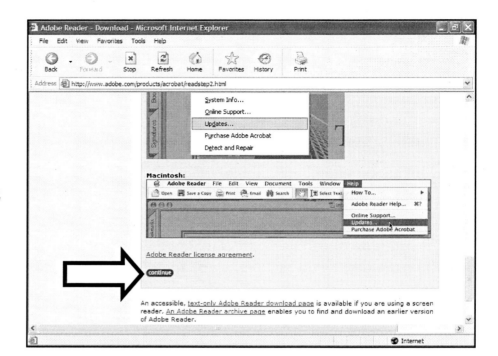

Step 2: Click the DOWNLOAD button.

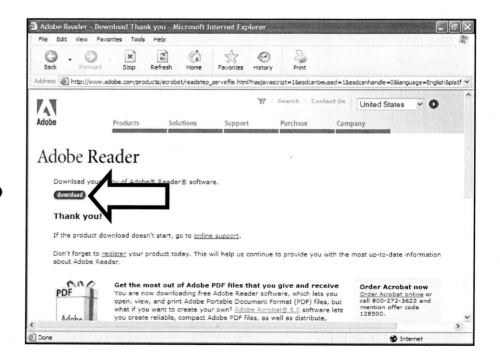

Step 3:
Click the SAVE
button.

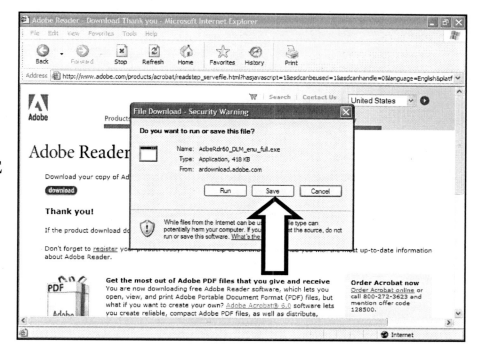

Step 4:
In the "Save In"
box, choose the
location in which
you would like to
save the
program.
(*Desktop*)

Make sure you
remember the
File Name of the
downloaded
program.

Step 5:
Click the SAVE
button.

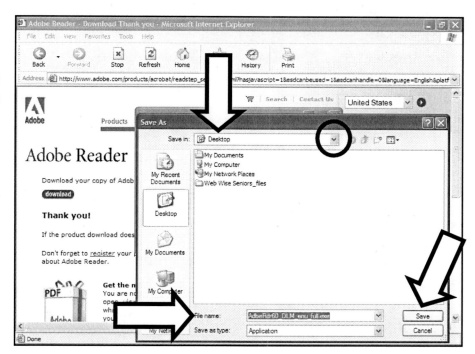

Progress window displays the rate of the file transfer.

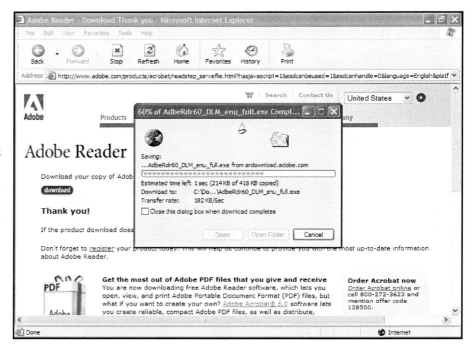

Step 6: Click the CLOSE button on the progress window.

Step 7: Click the MINIMIZE (-) button to hide the browser window.

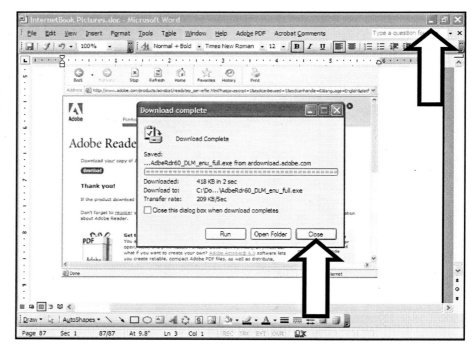

Locate the newly downloaded program and open the file.

A new icon for the downloaded program can be found on the Desktop.

Section 19: Installation

Installing New Software

Anytime you want to put a new program onto your computer, you have Install that program. Installation is the process of taking a new item (i.e., the downloaded program) and telling the computer how to use it.

There are two basic types of installations. You can install "hardware" or you can install "software." Installing hardware means adding a piece of equipment to your computer such as a printer, fax, or scanner. Installing software means adding a program to your computer such as a game, word processing program, or instructions for your computer which tell it how to use a new piece of equipment.

Most programs are installed by compact disk (CD). If you go to the store and buy a new program for your computer, you will come home with a CD containing the program. The CD contains the information necessary for your computer to interact correctly with the new software. You can also get a program by downloading it from the Internet, just like we did in the previous section. Instead of using a CD to complete the installation process, you need to open the downloaded file (by double clicking on its icon.) We will be showing you how to install the program (Adobe Reader) we just downloaded to our computer. The following section will provide you with guidelines for installing programs to your computer.

The Installation Process

The installation process may vary depending upon what you are installing to your computer. We are providing general guidelines that will help you get through the process.

WARNING: When installing software, make sure that NO programs are running on the computer. You do not want any games or half written letters open on your computer. If you begin installing a program to your computer and you have other programs running at the same time, you may cause errors to occur in the installation process.

Locate the file you just downloaded to your computer (Adobe Reader.) You saved it to the computer's Desktop. Double-click the icon (picture) to open the file and begin the installation process. After you open the file, read and follow the directions which appear on the computer screen. In 90% of installations, the only thing you need to do is to use your mouse to click on the OK or "Next" button. In general, the computer will tell you what to do. If you do not know what a particular screen is asking, do not worry. In most cases, the computer has already answered the question and is just asking you to confirm its choice. Simply click the OK or "Next" button.

The computer will tell you when it has finished installing your new program. When it has finished, restart your computer unless the computer tells you differently. Once again, the most important part of installation is remembering to read each window that appears on the computer screen during installation and following the directions.

Chapter 9: Downloading & Installation!

To help illustrate the installation process you will install Adobe Reader. This is the program we just downloaded onto the computer.

HINT: In the Installation process, OK buttons perform the same function as the "Next" button.

Installation Process: Step by Step Instructions

1. **Locate the program you want to Install.**
   - **Put in the CD.**
   - **Find the icon of the downloaded program. Double-click on the icon to open the downloaded file.**
2. **The computer will begin to unpack the program files. It will also open the installation wizard (question screens). Be patient, the installation setup wizard will prompt you when it needs help.**
3. **Click the NEXT button located on the introduction screen of the installation setup wizard.**
4. **The installation wizard will indicate that the new program is going to be loaded on the computer. To verify this, click the NEXT button.**
5. **The next screen asks you where you want to install the new information. In which part of the computer do you want to store your new program? The computer always answers this question for you. Unless you are a super experienced computer user, you do not want to adjust this information. The computer just wants you to acknowledge its choice. Click the NEXT button.**
6. **The computer needs to verify that you want to install the program. Click the INSTALL button to indicate acceptance.**
7. **Once Adobe Acrobat Reader is installed, the setup box will say that it is complete. Click the FINISH button.**
   - **The computer will return you to the Desktop. You will see a new icon. This icon allows you to open the program. You will also be able to open the program from the Start Menu.**

Installation Process: Visual Guide

Step 1:
Locate the
downloaded file
on the Desktop.

Double-click on
the file's icon.

Step 2:
The computer
will begin the
installation
process.

The computer is unpacking the program files and installation setup wizard.

The installation setup wizard will prompt you when it needs help.

Be patient while the program unpacks the program files.

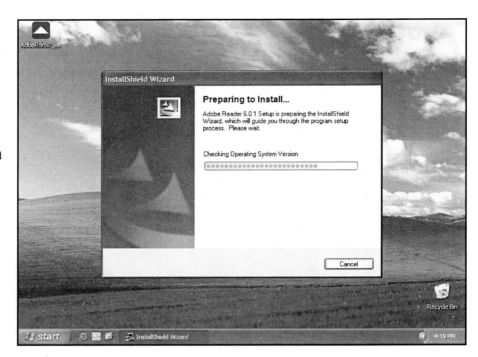

The installation setup wizard is preparing to open.

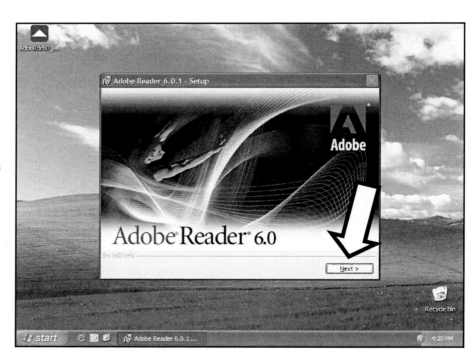

Step 3:
Click the NEXT button.

Step 4:
Click the NEXT
button.

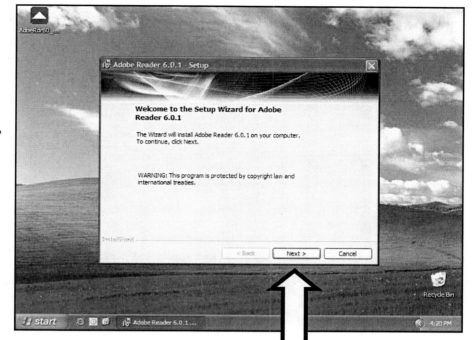

Step 5:
Click the NEXT
button.

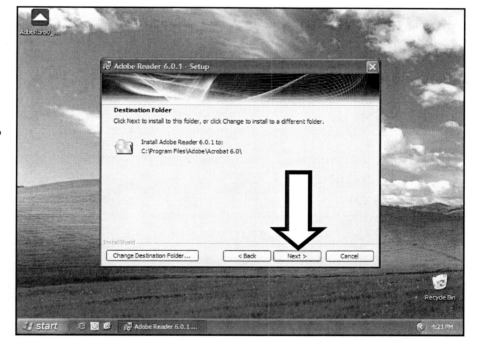

Step 6: Click the INSTALL button.

This screen confirms, a second time, that you want to Install the program.

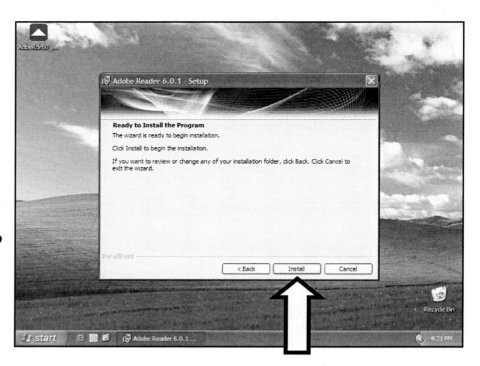

The computer is finishing the installation process.

The installation wizard will add the new program to the Start Menu and place a new icon on the Desktop.

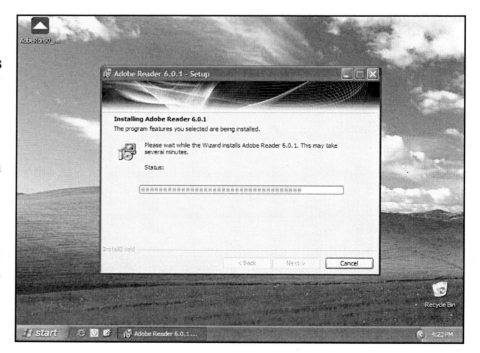

Step 7:
Click the
FINISH button.

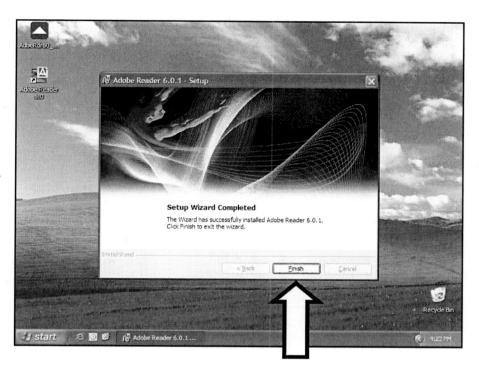

Locate the new
program icon
on the Desktop.

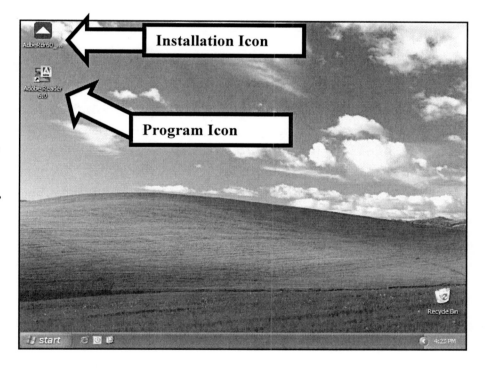

Installation Icon

Program Icon

Section 20:   Opening an Installed Program

Opening the Program

Once the program has been downloaded and installed, it is ready to use. The program can be accessed through either the Start Menu or the Desktop icon. To open the program using the Desktop icon, position the mouse over the picture (icon) for the program and double-click the left mouse button. The program will open. The first time a program is opened, a license agreement will be displayed. If you accept the licensing agreement, you are promising that you will not resell the program or use it for illegal purposes. You have to accept the agreement to use the program. If you do not accept the agreement, the program will not work.

Open the Newly Installed Program: Step by Step Instructions
1. Locate the program's icon on the Desktop.
2. Double-click on the icon to open the program.
    *   A window will appear displaying the program's license agreement.
3. Click the ACCEPT button.

Open the Newly Installed Program: Visual Guide

Step 1:
Locate the
program icon
on the Desktop.

Step 2:
Double-click on
the icon to open
program.

The program
will open.

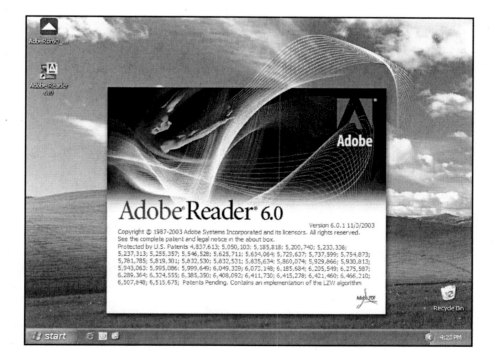

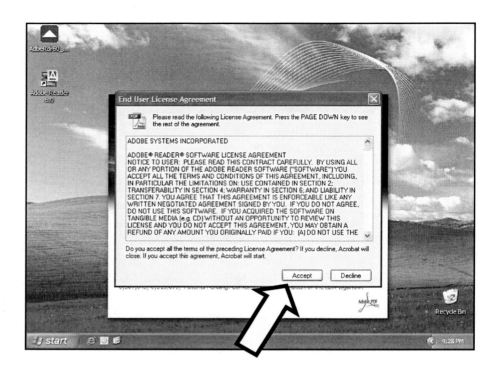

**Step 3:
Click the
ACCEPT
button.**

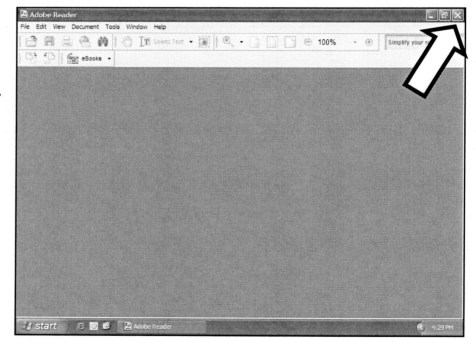

**An Adobe
Acrobat Reader
window will
open.**

**Click the Close
(X) button to
close the
window.**

Section 21: Removing a Desktop Icon

The installation process has completely saved all necessary information to the computer. Therefore, once the program has been installed, there is no need to keep the downloaded file. You can erase the file easily by using the click and drag method. Position the mouse pointer over the picture (icon) for the downloaded installation file (**not** the program icon). Click and hold down the left mouse button. The icon will turn blue. While holding down the mouse button, move the mouse over the recycle bin icon. Release the mouse button and the downloaded installation file will be moved into the trash.

Deleting a Desktop Icon: Step by Step Instructions

1. **Place your mouse arrow over the object that you want to erase.**
2. **Click the left mouse button and hold it down.**
   - **While holding the left mouse button down, move your mouse arrow to the Recycle Bin.**
3. **When you arrive at the Recycle Bin, release the left mouse button. The icon will be placed in the trash.**

Deleting a Desktop Icon: Visual Guide

Step 1:
Place your
mouse arrow
over the object
that you want
to erase.

In this
example, you
will place your
mouse arrow
over the
installation
icon.

Step 2:
Click the left
mouse button
and hold it
down.

While holding
the left mouse
button down,
move your
mouse arrow to
the destination.

The object will
follow.

Step 3:
When you arrive at the Recycle Bin, release the left mouse button.

The object will be dropped.

Section 22: Downloading RealPlayer®

RealPlayer

RealPlayer® is a music and video program for the computer. You can listen to music and watch videos right on your computer. The program is also very useful in transferring music to portable music players. RealPlayer® was created by RealNetworks and is available in two versions. Today, download the free player. If you later decide you would like more functionality, you can download the more advanced player.

The first thing you need to do is perform a specific search to locate the RealNetwork's website. Open the browser. (You minimized the screen, so it should be located in your toolbar, at the bottom of your screen.) Place your mouse pointer in the browser's address bar. Click the left mouse button once. Everything in the address bar will turn blue. Press the backspace button located on the keyboard. The web address will disappear. Now, type the address for the RealNetworks' website (www.real.com) in the address bar. When you are finished typing, press the enter key on the keyboard. The computer will open the website.

Specific Search: Step by Step Instructions

1. **Position the mouse pointer over the input box located in the address line.**
2. **Click the left mouse button one time.**
3. **Press the backspace key or the delete key on the keyboard to erase the highlighted text.**
4. **Type the new website address in the input box.**
   - **Example: www.real.com**
5. **Press the Enter Key on your keyboard to go to the website.**

Specific Search: Visual Guide

Obtain a website address. www.real.com

Step 1: Position the mouse pointer in the address line.

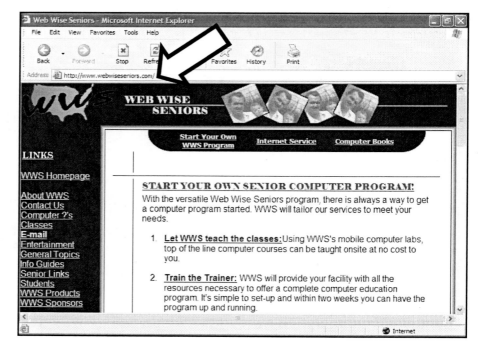

Step 2:
Click the left mouse button one time.

Step 3:
Press the backspace key on the keyboard.

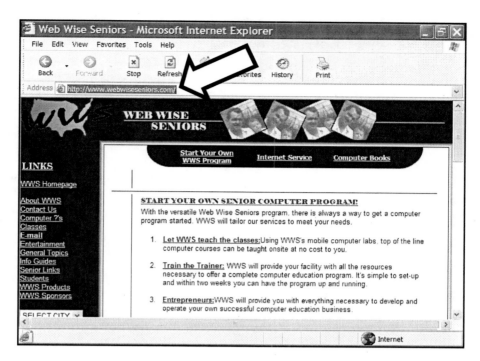

Step 4:
Type the new website address in the input box.

Step 5:
Press the Enter Key on your keyboard.

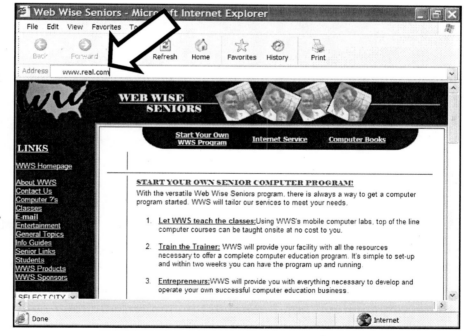

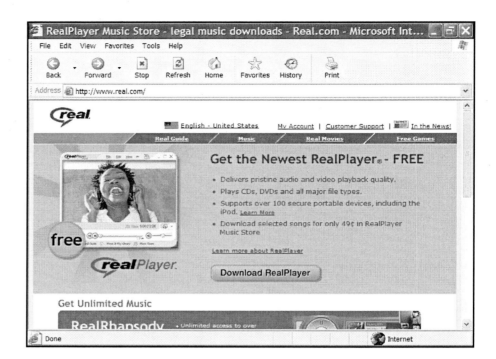

The Real Website.

The next thing you need to do is find the item you wish to download from the website. Read the instructions and make sure you are downloading the correct program. For the example, make sure you are downloading the free RealPlayer® program, not the more advanced one. After you have clicked the link to start the download, a window will appear asking you to begin downloading. Instead of saving the entire installation file to the computer, as we did in Adobe Reader, RealPlayer® will begin transferring the file immediately, as well as, beginning the installation process. Many people forget to erase the downloaded programs file once the program is installed. Since both processes are happening at once, you do not have to worry about it. This process also saves you room on the computer. Select the RUN option. A new screen will appear verifying you want to install the program. Select the Run option in the new message box and the process will begin. Be patient. Depending on the type of Internet connection you have, the download process may take a while to complete.

Chapter 9: Downloading & Installation!

Downloading from the Internet: Step by Step Instructions

1. Find the program on the Internet.
2. Click the link that indicates Download.
3. Click the option RUN located on the message box to run the executable file to process the download.
4. Click the option RUN located on the message box to run the installation program to instruct the computer how to use the program.

Downloading from the Internet: Visual Guide

Step 1:
Find the
program on the
Internet.

Step 2:
Click the link
"Download
RealPlayer®".

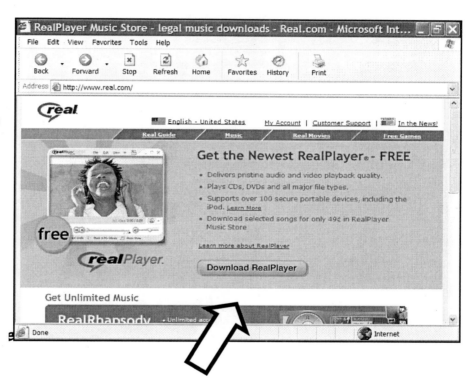

Chapter 9: Downloading & Installation!

Read the program description.

Scroll down and continue reading the program description.

Then click the DOWNLOAD FREE link.

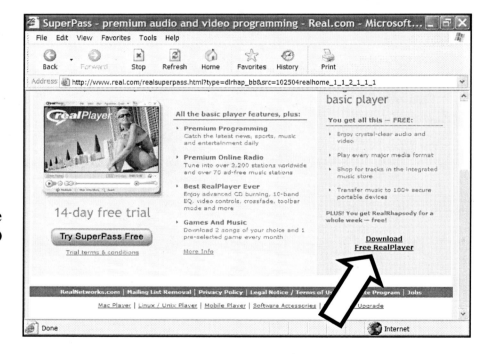

**Step 3:
Read the
download
instructions
before you
click the "Start
RealPlayer
Download"
link.**

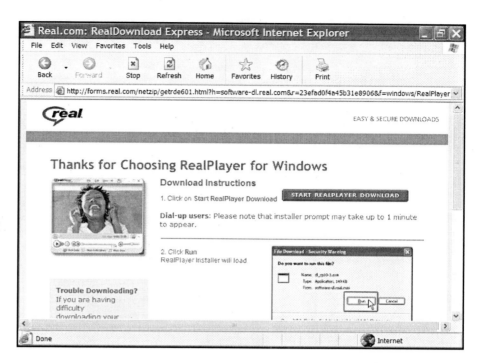

**Scroll down to
finish reading
the download
instructions.**

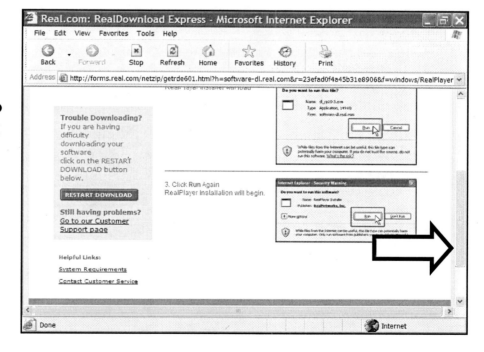

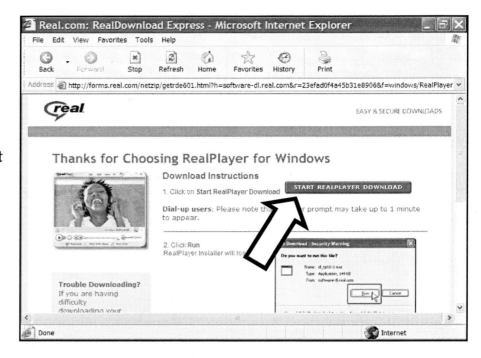

Scroll back up the page to click the "Start RealPlayer Download" link.

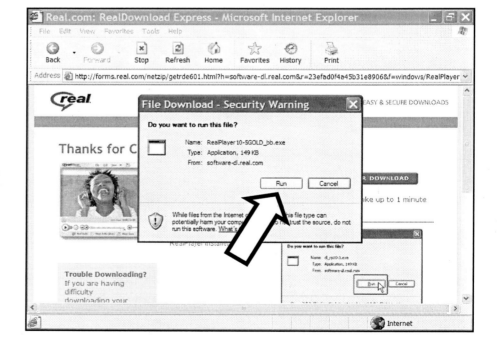

Step 4: Click the option RUN.

**Step 5:
Click the
option RUN.**

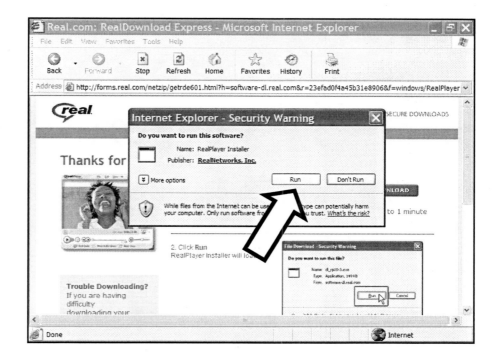

**Be patient
while the files
download.**

**Once the
download is
complete, the
installation
process will
automatically
begin.**

Download is complete.

The installation program will instruct the computer how to interact with the new program.

Section 23: Installing RealPlayer®

The creators of the RealPlayer® have instructed the computer to automatically begin the installation process after the files have finished downloading. At this point, your job is to read and follow the directions that appear on the computer screen. In 90% of installations, all you have to do is click on the OK or "Next" buttons as the computer moves through the installation process. During this process, RealNetworks will instruct you to read their license agreement and accept the terms. Basically, you are agreeing to use the program yourself without selling it or breaking any laws. If you do not accept the agreement, you will not be able to use the program.

Installation Process: Step by Step Instructions

1. Click the ACCEPT button pertaining to the License Agreement.
2. The next screen tells you where the program files will be saved. It also gives you the option to limit the number of new icons placed on your Desktop. Click on each check box, except for the shortcut to the RealPlayer® program. The check marks should disappear from each box, except for the first one.
3. Click the NEXT button.
4. Click the FINISH button.
   - The computer will automatically open the new program to finish the program setup.

Installation Process: Visual Guide

Step 1:
Read the
License
Agreement.
Click the
ACCEPT
button.

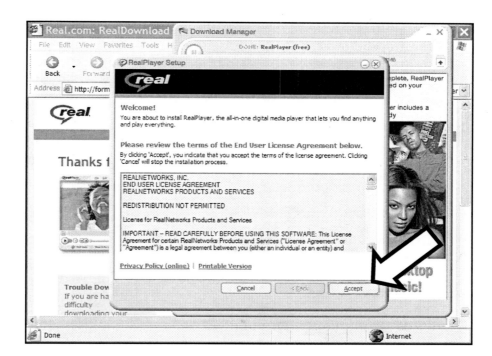

Step 2:
Click on each check box, except for the shortcut to the Real Player program.

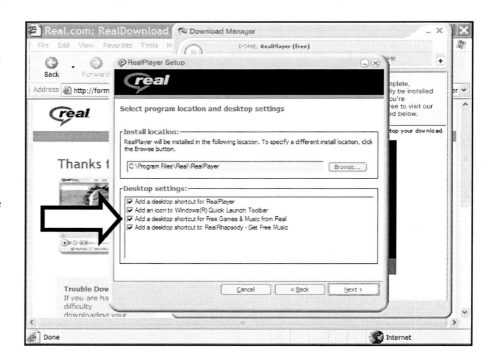

Step 3:
Click the NEXT button.

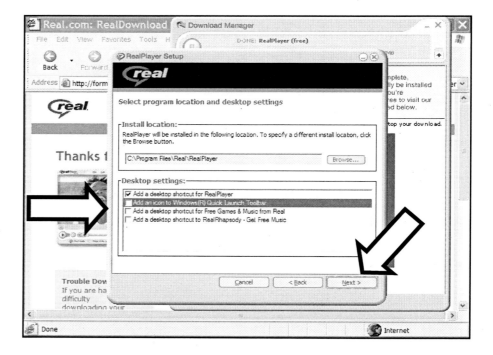

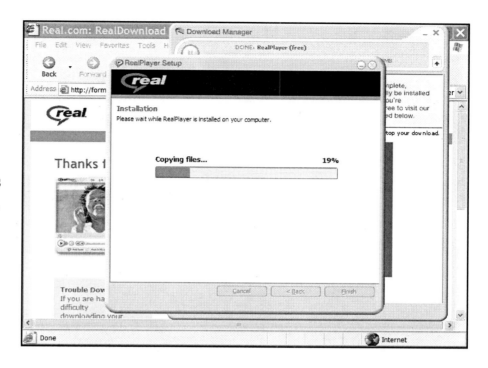

The files will be copied to the computer's main memory.

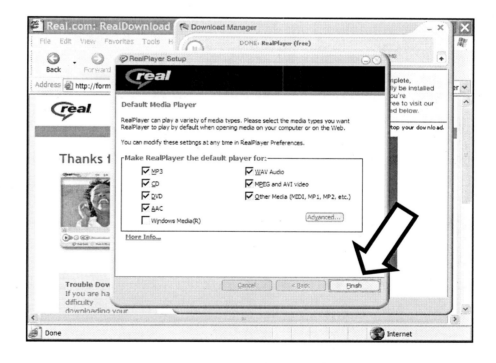

Step 4: Click the FINISH button.

To finish the setup, the program will connect to the company's computer system. After establishing a connection, the program will ask you if you want to load a new Google toolbar to the browser window. Decline the offer. Click the dot next to the option "Do Not Include the Google Toolbar." Click the "Continue" button.

The program creator, RealNetworks, will request information about the person who has downloaded the program. This information helps the company identify its user-base and provide better services in the future. Provide the requested information by typing in the input boxes provided. Remember to click the mouse in each box to activate it before typing. RealNetworks will also ask permission to contact you as new updates and products become available. You can refuse additional contact by clicking your mouse on the check boxes located at the bottom of the web page. The check mark will disappear from the box. Click the "Create" button to move to the final step of the setup process.

The final step of the setup process is to confirm your desire to use the free version of the RealPlayer® program. Click the circle next to the option "Basic Setup." A dot will appear in the circle. Click the "Continue" button to finish the setup process. The RealPlayer® window will automatically open after the setup is complete.

Setup Process: Step by Step Instructions
1. **Click the circle next to the "Do Not Include the Google Toolbar" option. A dot will appear in the box.**
2. **Click the CONTINUE button.**
3. **Type in the information requested in the input boxes provided.**
4. **Uncheck the boxes asking if you want to receive additional information. The checks will disappear.**
5. **Click the CREATE button.**
6. **Click the circle next to the option "Basic Setup." A dot will appear in the box.**
7. **Click the CONTINUE button.**

Setup Process: Visual Guide

The installation connects to the company's website in order to finish the setup process.

Step 1: Click the circle next to the "Do Not Include the Google Toolbar" option.

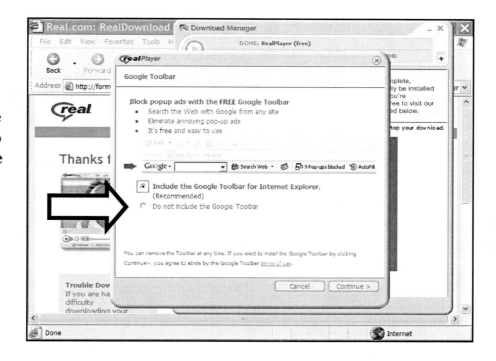

Step 2: Click the CONTINUE button.

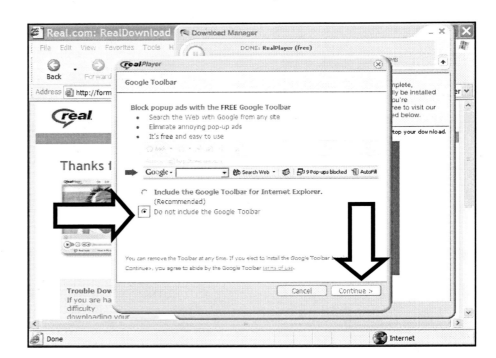

Step 3: Type the requested information into the input boxes.

Step 4: Uncheck the boxes asking if you want to receive additional information.

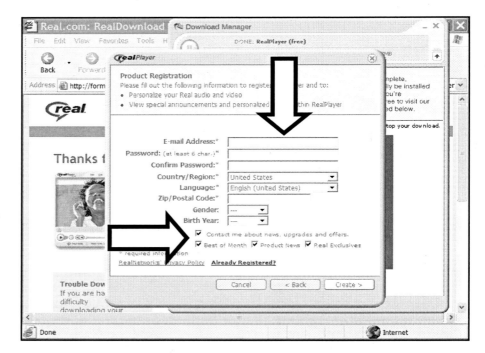

**Step 5:
Click the
CREATE
button.**

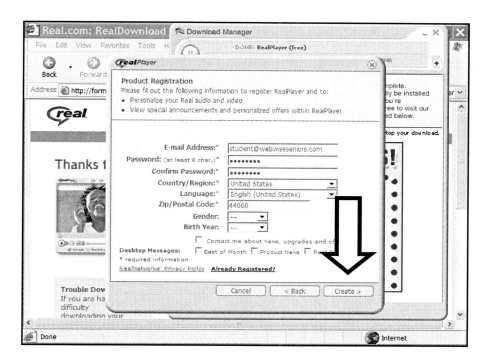

**Step 6:
Click the circle
next to the
option "Basic
Setup." A dot
will appear in
the circle.**

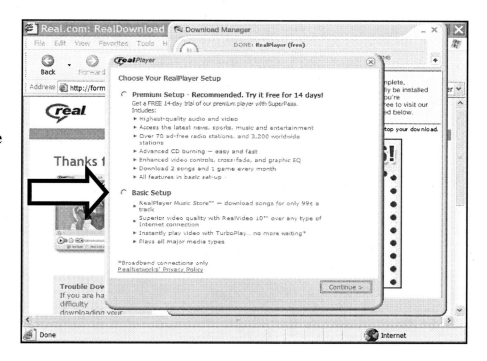

**Step 7:
Click the
CONTINUE
button.**

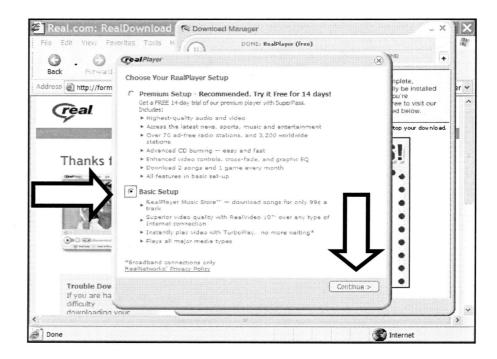

**The setup
process is
complete.**

**Step 8:
Click the Close
(X) button to
exit the
RealPlayer®
window.**

Step 9:
Click the Close
(X) button to
exit the
Installation
window.

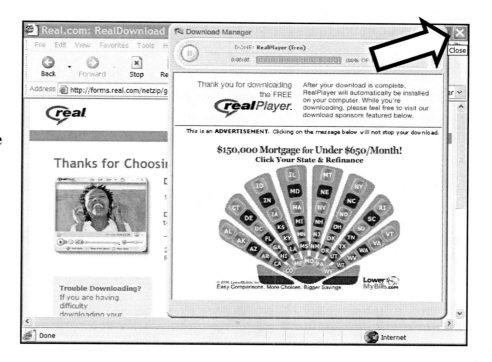

Step 10:
Click the Close
(X) button to
exit the
browser
window.

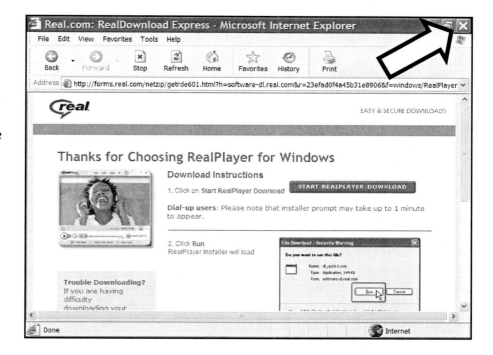

The new
RealPlayer®
icon is now
available on
the Desktop.

Chapter 10

Advertising on the Internet!

What You Will Learn in this Chapter
✓ How do companies advertise on the Internet?
✓ What is a banner ad?
✓ What is a pop-up ad?
✓ What are some advertising gimmicks?
✓ What are Adware, Spyware, and Sneakware?
✓ How to protect yourself from unethical advertising techniques.

Section 24: Advertising on the Internet

Most of the information on the Internet is free to the public. This currently includes search engines, some online newspapers, news resources, e-mail, and instant messenger programs, just to name a few. Websites can afford to offer these items for free because the advertising revenue they generate takes the place of user paid fees.

Advertising is done through sponsored links, banner ads, and pop-up advertisements. The objective is to inform and draw people to websites related to the company or product. Sponsored links are often found on search engine result pages. The sponsored links take you directly to the advertiser's website. For example, both Google and Yahoo have sponsor links running down the right side of their results list. Banner ads are small pictures or video clips which appear on a web page. Banner ads are the most commonly used Internet advertising method. Click the left mouse button on a banner ad and the advertiser's website opens.

Do not be fooled by gimmicks - these ads are supposed to be enticing. For example, some ads say hit the target and win. The target will be moving quickly back and forth across the screen. Clicking on the ad (the target) will result in opening the company's website. These "contests" are just advertisements. Most advertisers pay the website owner every time someone clicks of their advertisement.

Many Internet users have a tendency to ignore banner ads and sponsored links. So, to make sure their ads are being seen, some advertisers have implemented the use of pop-up advertisements. Pop-up ads open up in new windows, typically in front of the current browser window. These ads automatically open when a new web page is opened. Pop-up ads command your attention because you need to click on the ad's close (X) button in order to remove them. Advertisers like pop-up ads because they force Internet users to look and interact with the ad.

Internet advertisements are exactly like television commercials. They are annoying, but these ads keep the information on the Internet free for the public. Unfortunately, these ads have become an integral part of Internet experience.

Sponsor Link Advertising

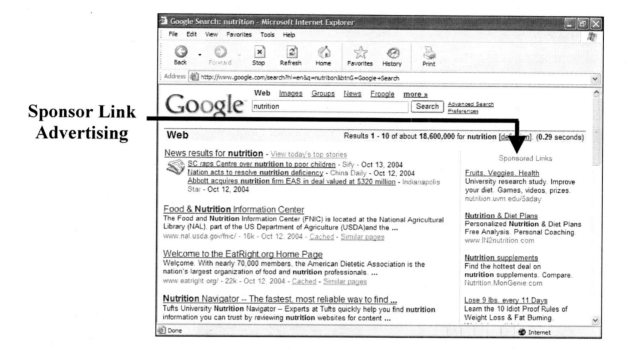

Chapter 10: Advertising on the Internet!

Banner Advertising

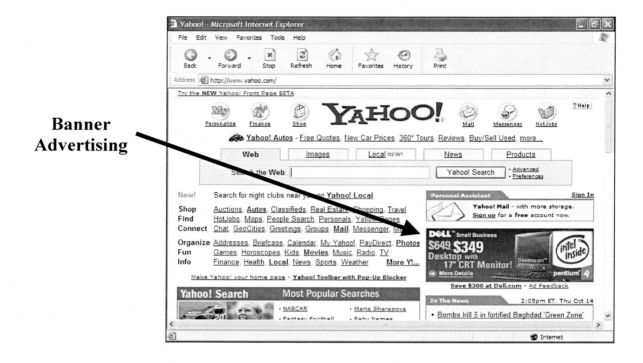

Pop-up Ad Advertising

NOTE: Not all pop-up windows are advertising! Some website designers use pop-up windows to retrieve information or to direct you to a third party website.

Advertising Gimmicks

Some pop-up ads are very enticing. Here are a few tricks and catch phrases commonly used on pop-ups:

- You're a winner!
- Urgent – update your computer now!
- FREE!
- You have a message waiting for you!

If you received an offer like one of these in your mail box at home, you would probably throw the ad straight into the trash without ever opening the envelope. Treat on-line offers in the same manner.

A few advertisers even use deceptive ads to illicit customers. These advertisers design their ads to look like a Windows message box. The ads are still just links to their website. You can use the mouse to decipher a real Windows message from an advertisement. Place the mouse pointer over a questionable item. If the mouse changes from a pointer into a hand, this is an indication that the box is an ad (a link to the company's website.) If the mouse pointer remains an arrow, it is probably a real Windows message. Pay attention to the mouse pointer before you click!

Section 25:   Internet Scams and Unwanted Advertising

What is Phishing?

Phishing is a scam that uses pop-up messages to deceive Internet users into disclosing credit card numbers, bank account information, social security numbers, passwords, or other sensitive information. The pop-up window/message might appear to be from a company you know and trust, but it is not. Most of these messages request urgent verification of your personal information. Con artists then collect your information instead of sending it to the real company. How do you know if a message is real or not? Well, when most legitimate institutions need information, they will call or send a letter. It is unlikely that they would use the Internet. If you suspect something may be a scam, call the company using a telephone number from the phone book or from a previous billing statement.

What is Adware?

Adware is unwanted advertising software that gathers information to track your Internet habits. Once an interest has been established, the program then opens pop-up ads which deal with these activities. For example, you may be researching mortgage rates on-line, and within a short time, you begin receiving pop-up ads from mortgage companies from whom you have not requested information. You have been a casualty of Adware.

What is Spyware?

Spyware is a program that retrieves confidential information from your computer and then transmits it back to the organization that planted it on your computer. Spyware is typically installed without your knowledge and poses identity theft risks. One example of spyware is a keystroke logger. The program records all you've typed in an attempt to gather items including your social security number, credit card number, or bank account information.

What is Sneakware?

Sneakware is used to sneak onto your computer to make changes to your computer settings. Typical changes include changing your Home Page or adding a toolbar to the browser window. Unfortunately, sneakware is often attached to programs you download from the Internet. When you grant permission for the program to be installed, you may also be granting permission for a sneakware program. Read the License Agreements of all programs you download to ensure you know exactly what you are agreeing to.

Eliminating Adware, Spyware and Sneakware.

Many companies are coming to the aid of Internet users by creating programs to detect and remove these unwanted programs from the computer. Two popular programs used to combat this growing problem are Ad-aware by Lavasoft (www.lavasoftusa.com) and Search & Destroy by Spybot (www.safer-networking.org).

Each of these programs costs under $40, but each company also provides free trial versions of their programs. After the program is installed, scan your computer weekly. Remember to keep the software updated so it can detect the most recent evolutions of spyware, adware, and sneakware.

QUESTION: What is a trial version of a program?

ANSWER: A trial version of a program will run for a limited amount of time. This allows a computer user to try the software and see if you like it. If you do like the program, you will need to buy a more advanced version of the program after your trial period runs out. Remember, people created these programs to help protect your computer. You need to pay them for their time and effort. You do that by buying the program.

Chapter 10: Advertising on the Internet!

Chapter 11

Viruses!

What You Will Learn in this Chapter

✓ What are viruses?
✓ How are viruses spread?
✓ What is an Internet worm?
✓ How can you protect yourself from viruses and worms?
✓ How do you update Windows?
✓ What is a firewall?
✓ How do you start Windows firewall?

Chapter 11: Viruses!

Section 26:   Viruses

What are Viruses?

Viruses are programs that you DO NOT want that are added to the computer without your knowledge or consent! Computer viruses range from small, unobtrusive files which are annoying to others that are malicious and destructive! A computer virus can affect the computer in many ways; viruses can erase programs or computer files, track Internet activity, collect personal data stored on the computer (i.e. passwords), slow down your Internet connection speed, or change the browser's Home Page. Just like a human virus, a computer virus's main objective is to reproduce and spread to other computers.

How do you get Viruses?

Viruses get into the computer in many different ways. The most popular way viruses are spread is via e-mail attachments. People unknowingly send out e-mail messages attached to files which are infected with a computer virus. The computer file acts as the virus' host. When an infected e-mail attachment is opened, the virus is transferred to the computer. After the computer is infected, the virus will attempt to spread itself to other computers. Many viruses are designed to automatically send themselves to people in your e-mail address list. This just continues the cycle of infection.

Viruses have also been known to spread through Internet downloads. The virus will attach to a seemingly harmless program. When the program is downloaded, the virus is released onto the computer.

The last way viruses are spread is through infected files on a floppy disk or CD. When the files are opened, the virus is released.

Chapter 11: Viruses!

What is a Trojan Horse Virus?

A Trojan Horse is the term given to a destructive program that masquerades as a "good" application. For example, you could download a "free" screen-saver or music file which you intend to enjoy on the computer. What you do not know is that a virus is attached to the program. Remember the ancient city of Troy!

What are Worms?

A worm is a program that replicates itself over a computer network and usually performs malicious actions. A worm's most insidious characteristic is its ability to replicate and distribute itself to other computers. While viruses rely on attaching to another program, worms can replicate independently. They hide in a computer and create copies of themselves. The result can be a simple display in a text message, warning you of the intrusion, or in the worst cases, all the files on your hard drive will be renamed, overwritten, or erased! For example, the "ILOVEYOU" worm spread by sending itself to all e-mail contacts in the person's e-mail address book, repeatedly, and at scheduled intervals. This worm disabled some company computer systems until a fix was developed.

Virus Protection

An anti-virus program, such as Symantec's Norton AntiVirus or McAfee AntiVirus, is the first line of defense against viruses and worms. The anti-virus software scans your computer files regularly, looking for unusual changes in file size, programs that match the program's database of known viruses, suspicious e-mail attachments, and other warning signs. Keep your antivirus software running at all times and update it often because new viruses come out daily.

The second line of defense against infection is common sense. First, do not open e-mail from an unknown source. Delete it immediately. You never know what someone is sending you, especially if you do not know the sender. Second, if you get an e-mail containing an attachment that seems out of the ordinary, delete the whole message. Remember, some viruses spread using e-mail addresses stored in e-mail address books. If something looks strange, delete the message and then ask the person who sent the message if they sent it. If it was important, ask them to send it to you again. Third, do not download programs or files from a website unless you know and trust the source.

Chapter 11: Viruses!

Keeping these ideas in mind will help protect you, your computer, and the files saved on it. Treat websites with the same common sense and caution you would show to any other stranger asking you for money or personal information, or offering a get rich quick "opportunity." If it looks too good to be true, it probably is.

Keep your computer software up to date. Updates will block many of the security holes used by worms and viruses. Microsoft provides security patches for its programs including Windows, Outlook, and Internet Explorer. As problems are discovered in software, the creator provides fixes and new security patches. These updates are free and help keep your computer and information safe.

QUESTION: How do I check to see if there are updates available for my programs?

ANSWER: Microsoft provides all updates through its website. To check for updates, open the "All Programs" list available through the Start menu. Within the All Programs menu you will find the Windows Update option. The Windows Update option will connect your computer to Microsoft's website and check for updates. If updates are available, you will have the choice to update the computer.

Depending on how many updates need to be downloaded and installed, the update process may take a large amount of time to complete. Once the computer has started, it will do all the work. Microsoft recommends checking for new updates on a daily basis. Perform the update at a time when you can leave your computer connected to the Internet. Before the updates download, the computer will generate an approximate time limit for the updating process. If multiple updates are recommended, consider downloading them one at a time to shorten the process.

Updating Windows: Step by Step Instructions
1. Open the START menu.
2. Highlight ALL PROGRAMS.

3. Click the "Windows Update" option or do a specific search for http://windowsupdate.microsoft.com using the address bar of your Internet browser.

Updating Windows: Visual Guide

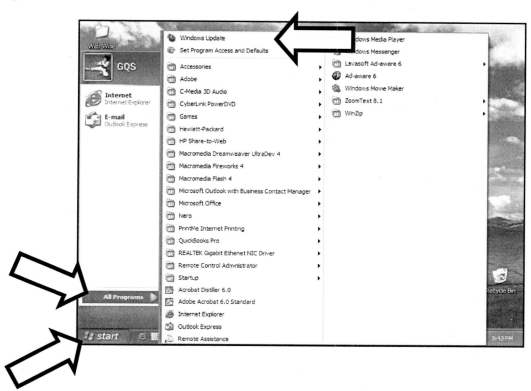

Section 27: Firewalls

A firewall is a system designed to protect a computer or network of computers from unauthorized access. In principle, think of a firewall as two security guards at a country club. One guard is there to prevent people from trespassing on the private property and the other is there to let authorized people enter. A firewall does both jobs. Unfortunately, there are people in the world that like to steal and destroy others' property. The firewall's job is to protect you from these people, while still enabling you to get your work done. To help protect your home computer, turn on the firewall built into Windows XP.

Turning on the Windows Firewall: Step by Step Instructions

1. **Open the START menu.**
2. **Click the CONTROL PANEL option.**
3. **Click the SECURITY CENTER option.**
4. **Double-click the WINDOWS FIREWALL icon.**
5. **Click the "On" (recommended) option.**
6. **For added security click the "Don't allow exceptions" check box.**
   - **Used for maximum protection, such as when a dangerous virus or worm is spreading over the Internet.**
7. **Click the OK button.**

Turning on the Windows Firewall: Visual Guide

Step 1:
Open the
START Menu.

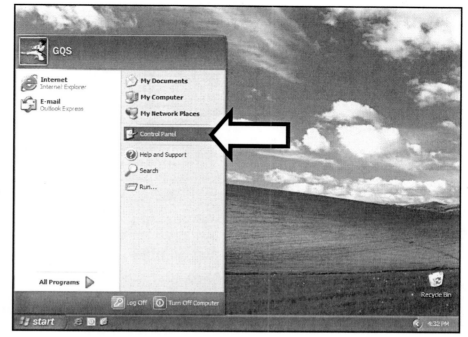

**Step 2:
Click the
CONTROL
PANEL option.**

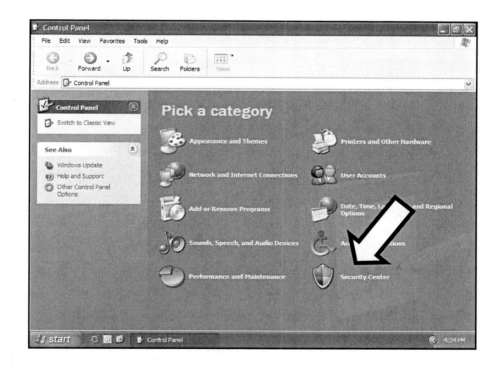

**Step 3:
Click the
SECURITY
CENTER
option.**

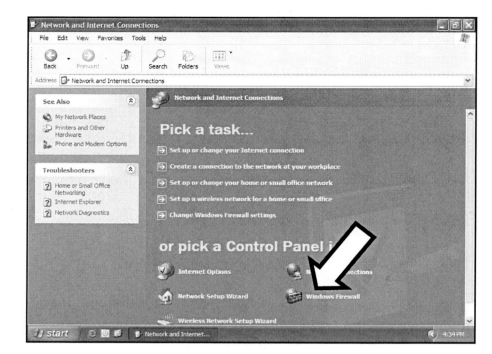

**Step 4:
Double-click
the
WINDOWS
FIREWALL
icon.**

**Step 5:
Click the "On"
option.**

**Step 6:
For added
security click
the "Don't
allow
exceptions"
check box.**

**Step 7:
Click the OK
button.**

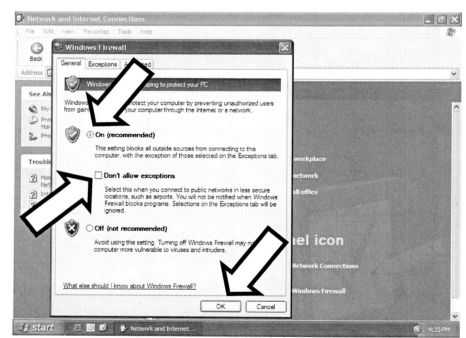

Chapter 11: Viruses!

If you have Windows 2000 or an earlier version, your computer probably does not have a firewall. You can install firewalls purchased from a third party vendor. Two firewalls for home use are Norton Personal Firewall (www.symantec.com) and ZoneAlarm (www.zonelabs.com). Each of these programs is under $50 and designed for a home computer.

With all of these potential hazards, it begins to feel like the Internet is a hostile and dangerous place and should be totally avoided. But the good news is, if you take certain precautions and use common sense, you can enjoy the Internet and its resources without worry.

Chapter 11: Viruses!

Chapter 12

Printing from the Internet!

What You Will Learn in this Chapter
✓ What is the printing process?
✓ How do you preview a page before it is printed?
✓ How do you print only part of a page?

Section 28:   Printing

The Printing Process

You can print a paper copy of information you find on the Internet if you have a printer connected to your computer. In order to print, you need to open the File menu. The File menu is located in the upper left corner of your Internet browser screen in the menu bar. Click your left mouse button on the word "File" to open the menu. Slide your mouse arrow down the File menu and click on the option "Print." The File menu will close and a Print screen will appear.

There are several important features on the print screen. At the top, you will see the name of your printer. On the left side of the screen is the page range. Page range shows you how many document pages will be printed. Remember, web pages are like Egyptian scrolls. One web page may take multiple pieces of paper to print. For example, a web page may look like only one page, but might use three pieces of paper when printed on 8x11 sheets of paper. Page range refers to the number of physical pages required to print the web page. For example, you can choose to print all of the web page's information or only a specific page (e.g. Page 1 equals the first page or top of the web page). The computer is set to automatically use the "ALL" option, meaning it will print the entire web page, regardless of the physical number of pieces of paper it will take.

If you do not want to print every page of your document, you have two options. You can choose to print only a selection of text or only specific pages of text. To print a selection of text, you must first highlight (turn blue) the section you desire. This option is very handy when you want to conserve ink and only need to print specific sections of a web page.

The second option, PAGES, permits you to type in the specific page number(s) of the page(s) to be printed. For example, if you only want to print the top of the web page, you can type "1" in the page number box. Only one physical piece of paper will be printed. If you want to print pages 1,3, and 5, type 1,3,5 in the input box. If you want to print pages 1 through 5, type 1-5 in the box.

The right side of the print screen contains the option "Number of Copies." This allows you to choose the number of times you want the computer to print the selected document or file. The computer has been programmed to print one copy. If you need more than one copy, you must change this option by clicking on the tiny up and down arrows located on the right side of the small white input box located to the right of the heading "Number of Copies." Each click of the tiny up and down arrows will change the number in the white input box.

Located just below the "Number of Copies" heading is another option called "Collate." The Collate option can be either checked (turned on) OR unchecked (turned off). The Collate option is only used if you are printing multiple copies of a web page. When collate is checked, the computer will print one full copy of the web page, then print the next full copy, and so on, with all pages in the proper sequence. If the Collate option is unchecked (off), the computer will print all the copies of page one, then all the copies of page two, then all the copies of page three, and so on. You will then have to put the copies in order manually. As you can see, making certain the Collate option is checked can save you a lot of time and effort.

After you choose the number of copies and the page range you want, click on the "Print" button located on the lower right side of the print screen. The print screen will close and your printer will make a paper copy of the web page.

Example Print screen.

Page Range Section on Left.

Number of Copies on Right.

PRINT button bottom center.

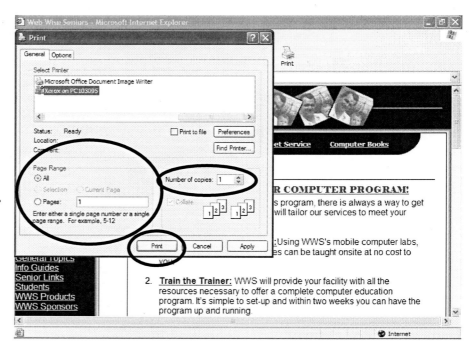

Printing a File (One Copy): Step by Step Instructions

1. Click on the FILE Menu.
2. Click the PRINT option.
3. Choose the Page Range and Number of Copies desired.
4. Click on the PRINT button.

Printing a File: Visual Guide

Step 1:
Click on the
FILE Menu.

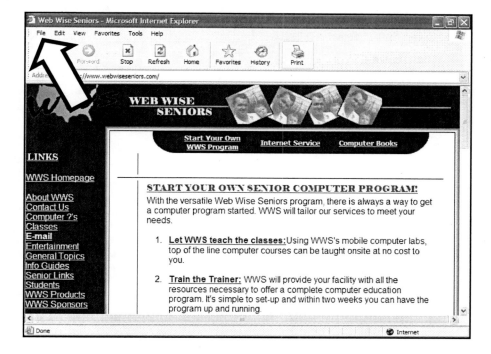

Step 2:
Click on the
PRINT option.

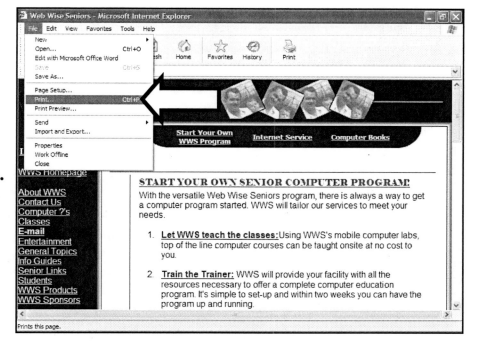

Step 3:
Choose the Page
Range and
Number of
Copies desired.

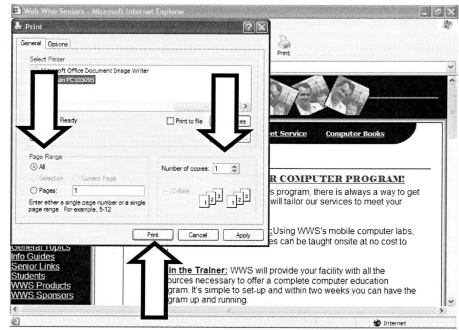

Step 4:
Click on the
PRINT button.

NOTE: The Print button located in the browser toolbar will automatically print the entire web page without opening the print window. To use the options found on the print screen, open the print screen by using the Print option located in the File menu.

Printing a File (Multiple Copies): Step by Step Instructions

1. Click on the FILE Menu.
2. Click the PRINT option.
3. (Optional): Select "Page Range" and "Number of Copies"
4. Make certain the COLLATE option has a check mark next to it.
5. Click on the PRINT button.

Printing a File (Multiple Copies): Visual Guide

**Step 1:
Click on the
FILE Menu.**

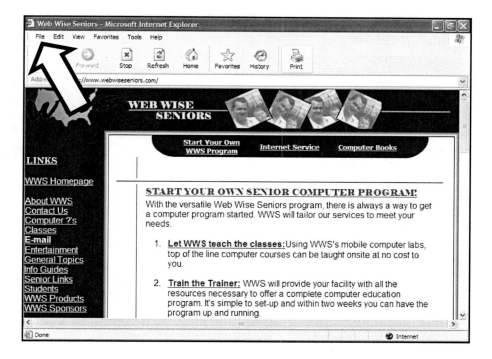

**Step 2:
Click on the
PRINT option.**

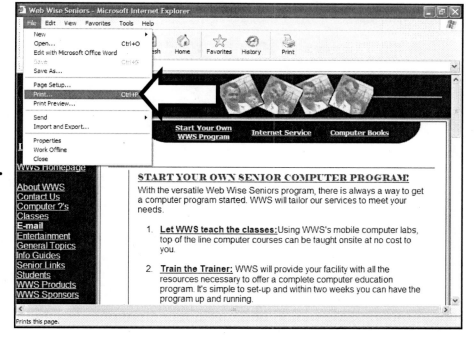

Step 3:
Select "Number of Copies"

Step 4:
Make certain the COLLATE option has a check mark next to it.

Step 5:
Click on the PRINT button.

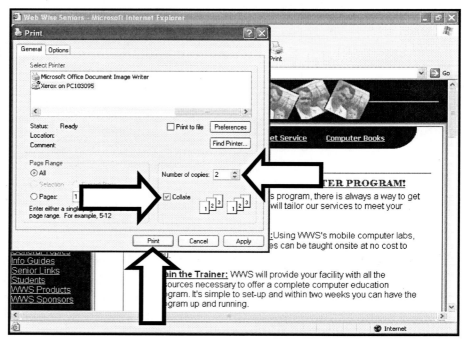

Section 29:   Print Preview

The Print Preview Option

Another helpful feature available through the Internet browser is the ability to see what a web page will look like when it is printed. The "Print Preview" option is located in the File menu. Clicking "Print Preview" will display a new screen showing you a zoomed out perspective of the printed page. It will enable you to see the entire page, including margins. The image displayed in this screen is exactly what will be printed out.

Chapter 12: Printing from the Internet!

Located at the top of the Print Preview screen is a helpful toolbar which enables you to change how you view the previewed document. This toolbar contains options that give you with the ability to zoom in and out, view multiple pages at once, and more. When you have finished looking at the preview screen, click on the word "Close" on the gray toolbar.

Opening Print Preview: Step by Step Instructions
1. **Click on the FILE menu.**
2. **Click on PRINT PREVIEW option.**

Opening Print Preview: Visual Guide

**Step 1:
Click on the
FILE Menu.**

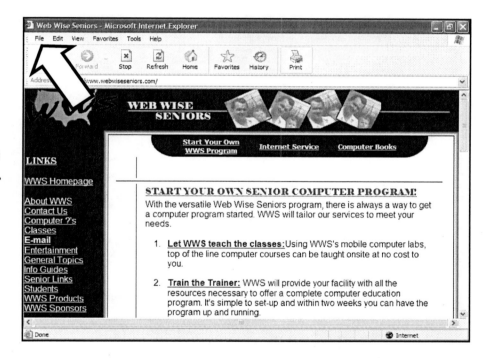

Chapter 12: Printing from the Internet!

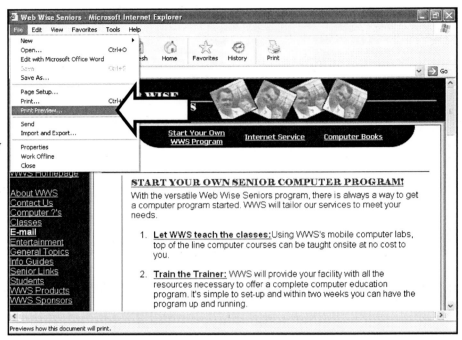

**Step 2:
Click on the
PRINT PREVIEW
option.**

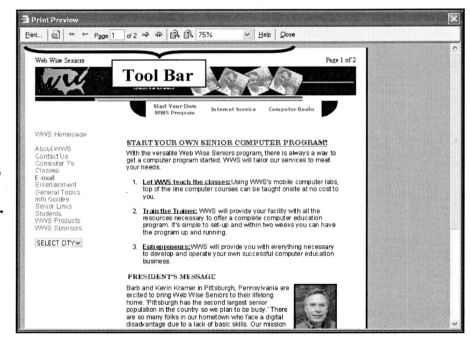

**Example of
Print Preview
Mode**

**The Tool bar
enables you to
change views
and print your
page.**

Print Preview toolbar options.

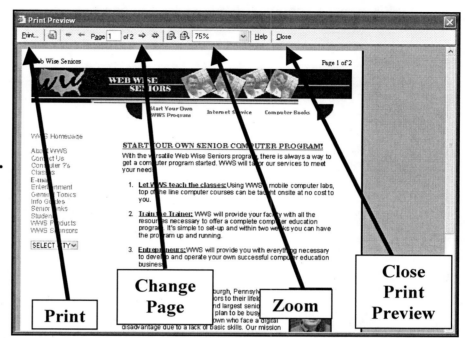

Section 30: Printing Only Part of a Page

The Print Selection Option

Printing web pages can be very costly and produce lots of waste. Many times you only need one paragraph or a small section of a web page, but, when you print the page, the entire page prints including the section you desire. To conserve paper and money, try highlighting a section of the web page and using the "Selection" option found on the print screen. Highlight the section you want to print. Open the print window by clicking the "Print" option located in the File menu. The Selection option is located under the page range heading. The Selection option will only be available if part of the web page is highlighted before opening the print screen.

Highlighting

Highlighting is used to tell the computer what specific part of the web page you want. Once a selection of text is highlighted, it may be copied or printed. To highlight text, position your mouse arrow at the end of the text you want to select. Click and HOLD DOWN the left mouse button. While holding down the mouse button, move your mouse arrow to the beginning of the text you want to select. As the mouse moves over the text, it will turn blue or black. This is called being highlighted. After reaching the beginning of the desired text, release the mouse button. The selected text will remain highlighted until you click in the display area again. The computer is now ready to work with your selected text.

When you highlight text, the computer is only concerned about the data between where you began holding down the left mouse button and the exact point at which you released the left mouse button. Think of these positions as two dots. Anything in between these dots will be highlighted. How you move from one location to another (left to right, or right to left) does not matter. The computer only focuses on the area between those two dots.

Now, try to highlight the first paragraph on the Web Wise Seniors website. (www.webwiseseniors.com) Position the mouse after the period at the end of the first paragraph. Click and hold down the left mouse button. Move your mouse across the text until it is positioned before the first word in the paragraph. The entire paragraph should have a black background. Release your mouse button.

WARNING: Don't release the left mouse button until the entire paragraph has been highlighted. Releasing the button will stop the highlighting process before you have included all the text. You will have to start the highlighting process over again.

The only thing more important than knowing how to highlight text, is knowing how to un-highlight text. If you accidentally highlight an area, simply click your mouse anywhere in the display area one time. A single click will remove all the highlighting on the page.

Highlighting Your Text: Step by Step Instructions
1. **Position the mouse at the end of the desired text.**
2. **Click and hold down the left mouse button.**
3. **Move the mouse to the beginning of the desired text.**
4. **Release the mouse button.**
   - The dark background indicates it has been highlighted.

Highlighting Your Text: Visual Guide

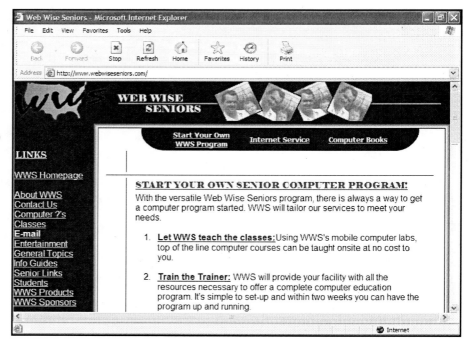

Open the Web Wise Seniors web page.

www. webwiseseniors .com

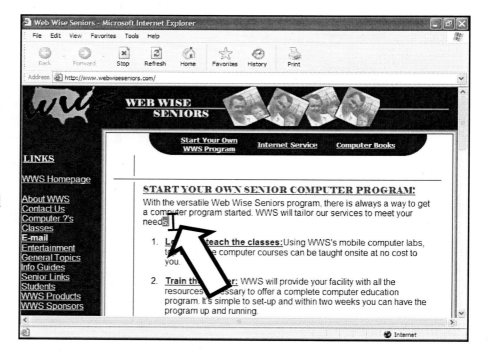

Step 1: Position the mouse at the end of the desired text.

Step 2: Click and hold down the left mouse button.

**Step 3:
Move the mouse
to the beginning
of the desired
text.**

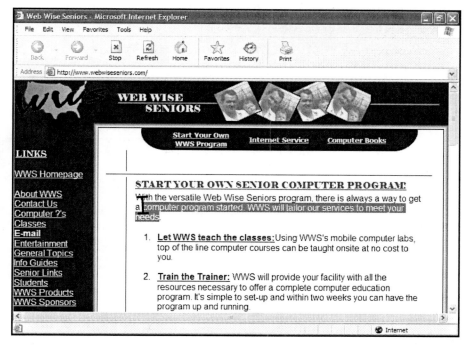

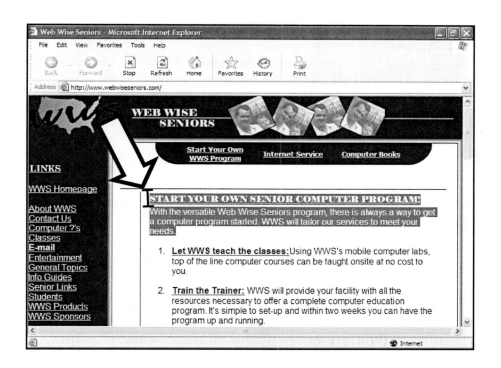

Chapter 12: Printing from the Internet!

Printing a Selection: Step by Step Instructions

1. Click on the FILE Menu.
2. Click the PRINT option.
3. Click the SELECTION option located under the Page Range heading.
4. Click on the PRINT button.

Printing a Selection: Visual Guide

Step 1:
Click on the
FILE Menu.

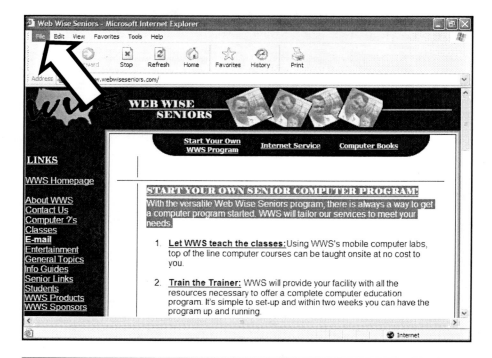

Step 2:
Click the
PRINT option.

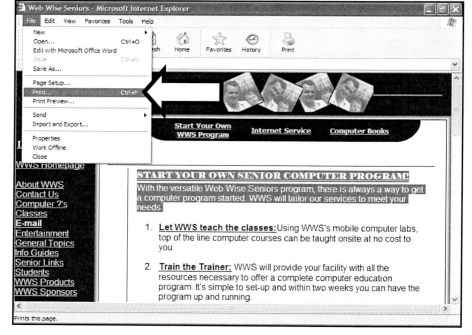

Step 3:
Click the
SELECTION
option located
under the Page
Range heading.

Step 4:
Click on the
PRINT button.

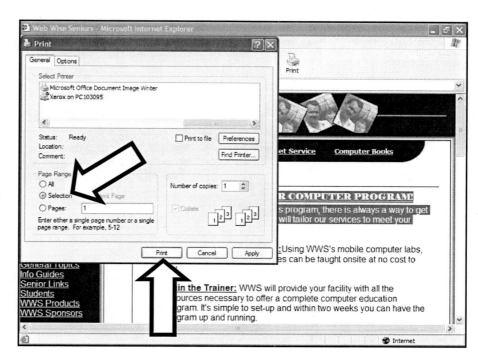

Un-highlight
the text.

Click the mouse
anywhere in the
display window.

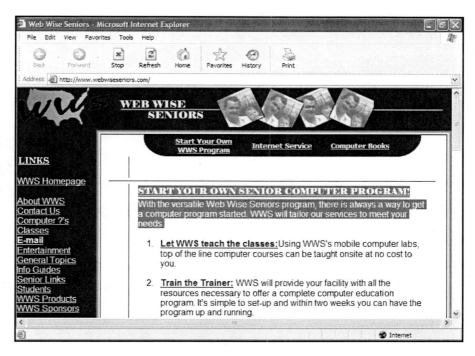

The text has been successfully un-highlighted.

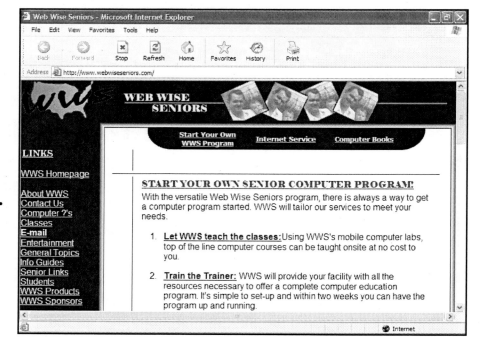

Chapter 13

Saving from the Internet!

What You Will Learn in this Chapter
✓ How do you save an Internet web page?
✓ How do you save a picture from the Internet?
✓ How do you save text from the Internet?

While searching the Internet, you may find data or images you would like to save for future use. Remember, data and images found on an Internet website are the property of the creator. Even though the computer will allow you to copy almost anything off of a website, be careful about how you use the item. Legally you do not own it. You can use the item for personal use, but it is illegal (plagiarism) to professionally use or sell another person's work unless you have permission.

Section 31:   Saving Items from the Internet

What Does the Term "Saving" Mean?

When you are using the Internet, each web page is stored in the computer's temporary memory while it is displayed by the browser. When the computer is shut off, the temporary memory is erased. This means, if you want to see the information on the web page again, you have to return to the web site. When you save something, the item is usually stored in your computer's main memory. Saving enables you to the view the item at a later time, on or off the Internet, without loss of information.

The saving process itself is not difficult. The hard part is remembering where you saved the files and what you named them, so you can find them easily in the future. Internet Explorer is set up to store all your text in a folder titled My Documents and all images in a folder titled My Pictures. These folders are located on the computer's main memory referred to as the Local Disk, C: drive, or hard drive. In the next few examples, you are going to save an entire web page, as well as a picture located on a web page.

Chapter 13: Saving from the Internet!

Saving a Web Page

Most people do not save websites to the computer. Most important websites are added to the Favorites list. This provides access to the page from its original location. When the site is opened from the Favorites list, any changes made by the web page designer will be shown. Saving the page to your computer takes a snapshot of the page and saves it to the computer's main memory. The snapshot remembers the information exactly as you viewed it.

To save a web page, display it in the browser window. For this example, open the Classes page located on the Web Wise Seniors' website (www.webwiseseniors.com). The link to Classes is located on the left side of the Web Wise Seniors Home Page. Once the page is displayed, you can begin the save process. Position the mouse arrow on the "FILE" menu located at the top of the browser window. Click the left mouse button once to open the menu. Move the mouse arrow down to the "SAVE AS" option and click the left mouse button. This closes the file menu and opens the save screen. There are three additional steps to complete the save process. First, you must choose where to save the file. Second, you have to give the file a name and, third, you must click the "SAVE" button.

First, you need to tell the computer where you want to save the file. At the top of the save screen is the heading "SAVE IN:" followed by a white box and a gray arrow pointing down. This gray arrow tells you that the box is a drop down menu. If you click on the gray arrow, a list will appear displaying the locations where you can save your file. If the white box currently displays "DESKTOP," you are in the right location. If it does not display "DESKTOP," you need to choose "DESKTOP" from the list.

To change the location to "DESKTOP," place your mouse arrow on the gray drop down arrow and click your left mouse button. Position the mouse arrow over the "DESKTOP" option from the drop down list that appears. It will turn blue. To make the selection, click the left mouse button. The list will close and "DESKTOP" will be displayed in the "Save In" box. You have now finished the first part of the save process.

The second step is to choose a name for the file. Located near the bottom of the save screen you will see the heading "FILE NAME." To the right of the heading "FILE NAME" will be a white input box containing a web page name. The name in the input box is the computer's suggestion for a name.

For this example, keep the name provided by the computer and move on to the third step of the save process.

NOTE: To change the suggested name, move your mouse arrow to the end of the name and click the left mouse button. Clicking the mouse activates the box and drops the cursor (blinking line) at the location the mouse was clicked. Use the backspace key on the keyboard to erase the suggested name. When the name has been erased, type in the desired name using the keyboard.

NOTE: When choosing a name, you can use up to 256 characters. The file name may include any numbers (0-9) and letters (A-Z), but not colons, semicolons, slashes, or mathematical operators (for example, the plus and minus signs). We recommend you use a maximum of three or four short words. If the name is too long, you will not see the full name when it is displayed in lists. By keeping it short, you have a better chance of seeing the entire name displayed when searching through the computer. This will help you later when you are looking for your work. If the name is too long, the computer will only show part of the name followed by three dots.

The final step in the saving process is to click the "SAVE" button located on the bottom right side of the save screen. When you click the "SAVE" button, the computer will close the save screen and the file will be successfully saved to the computer's main memory.

QUESTION: How do you know the web page was saved successfully?

Chapter 13: Saving from the Internet!

ANSWER: If you minimize the browser window, you will see a new icon located on the Desktop. This verifies the page was saved correctly.

Locate the example web page: Step by Step Instructions

1. Open the Web Wise Seniors website by doing a specific search using the website address: www.webwiseseniors.com
2. Click the link "Classes" located on the left side of the WWS page.

Saving a Web Page: Step by Step Instructions

1. Click on the FILE menu.
2. Click the SAVE AS option.
3. Locate the SAVE IN box and click the gray arrow to open the drop down list.
4. Click the option DESKTOP.
5. Locate the FILE NAME box and view the name of page.
6. Click the SAVE button.

Saving a Web Page: Visual Guide

Step 1:
Open the website address www. webwiseseniors .com

Step 2:
Click the link CLASSES.

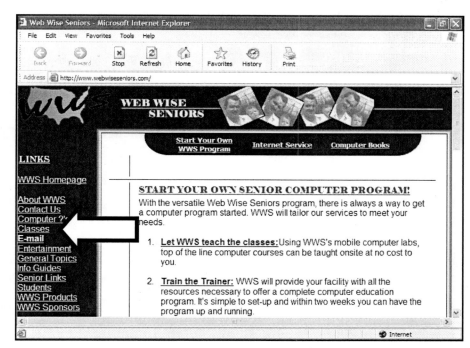

Chapter 13: Saving from the Internet!

Begin the Save Process

Step 1: Click on the FILE menu.

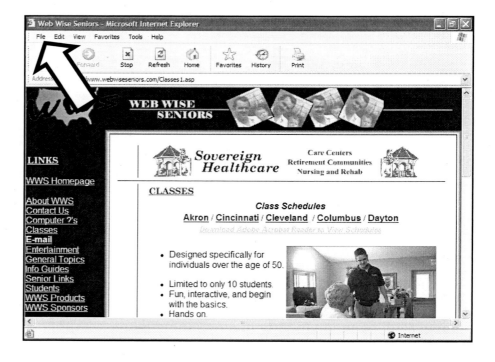

Step 2: Click the SAVE AS option.

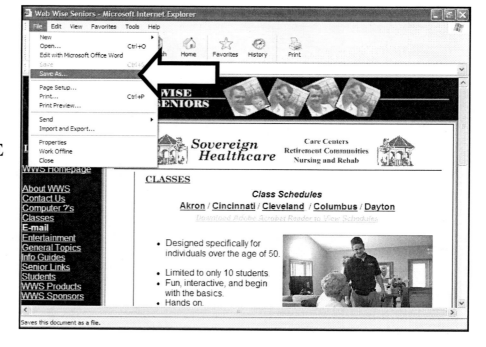

Step 3:
Locate the
SAVE IN box
and click the
gray arrow to
open the drop
down list.

Step 4:
Click the option
DESKTOP.

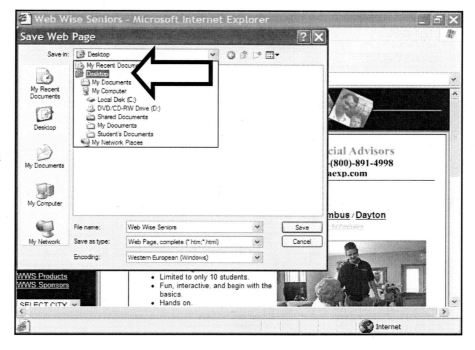

Step 5:
Locate the FILE
NAME box and
view the name
of the page.

Step 6:
Click the SAVE
button.

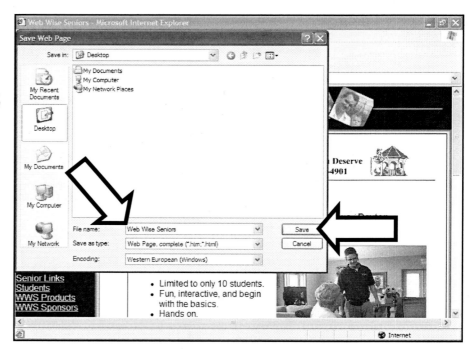

Verify the web
page was saved
successfully.

Click the
minimize button
to view the
Desktop.

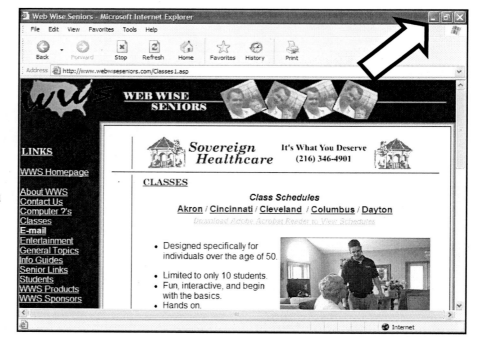

Chapter 13: Saving from the Internet!

Locate the icon for the saved web page.

Saving Pictures from the Internet

Often while browsing the Internet, you will find a picture you would like to save. Most images located on the Internet can be saved, but remember these images are the property of the creator. Typically, if you do not commercially reproduce or attempt to sell the image, you will not have any problems.

For this example, go to the Web Wise Seniors "Classes" page and view the first image. Try to scroll the page to view a large portion of the total picture. Position the mouse over the image and pause (approximately three seconds.) In the upper left corner of the picture, a toolbar will appear displaying options for working with the image. One of the options will be a small blue/gray floppy disk. This icon represents the save option. Move your mouse over the icon of the floppy disk and click the left mouse button. The save screen will open. There are three additional steps to complete the save process. First, you must choose where to save the file. Second, you have to give the file a name and, third, you must click the "SAVE" button.

If you are continuing from the last example (where we saved the web page) the browser window is already open, but currently minimized. Locate the browser button in the blue task bar located at the bottom of the Desktop.

Click the button with the name of your browser in it. The browser window will redisplay.

If you closed your browser, open the browser using the Start menu and do a specific search for www.webwiseseniors.com.

Locate the example web page: Step by Step Instructions
1. Open the Web Wise Seniors web site by doing a specific search using the website address. www.webwiseseniors.com
2. Click the Classes link located on the left side of the WWS page.

Saving Pictures: Step by Step Instructions
1. Find an image on the Internet.
2. Position the mouse over the image and pause for three seconds. The picture toolbar will appear.
3. Click the Save icon located in the picture toolbar. It is a picture of a small blue/gray disk. The save screen will appear.
4. Locate the SAVE IN box. The SAVE IN box should display the name "My Pictures."
5. Locate the FILE NAME box and view the name of picture. Either leave the currently displayed name in the box or type in a new name.
6. Click the SAVE button.

Saving Pictures: Visual Guide

Open the web site address. www. webwiseseniors .com

Click the CLASSES link.

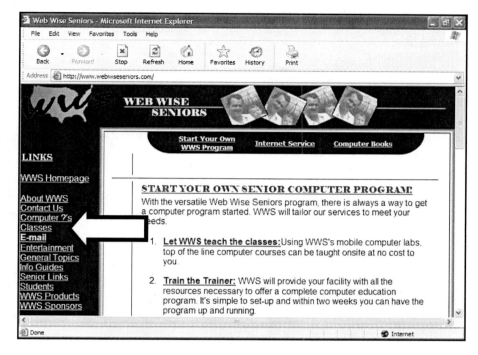

Step 1: Locate the desired image.

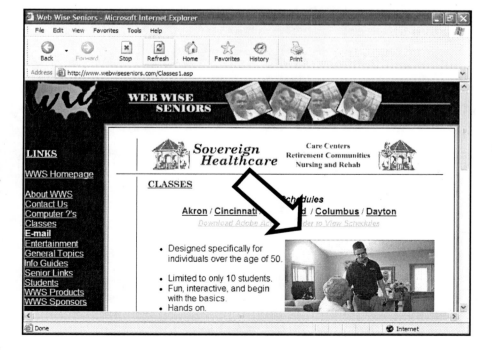

Scroll down to view the entire image.

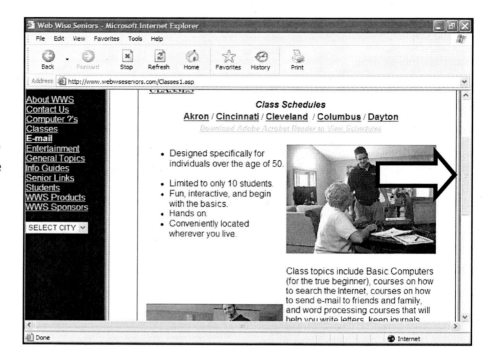

Step 2: Position the mouse over the image and pause for three seconds. The picture toolbar will appear.

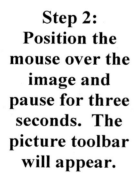

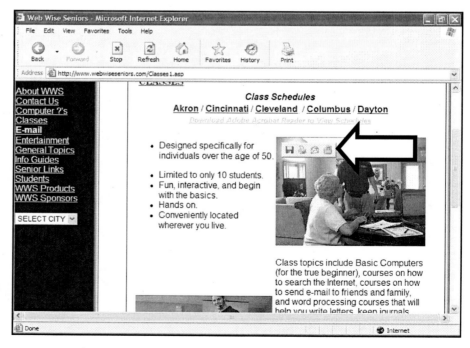

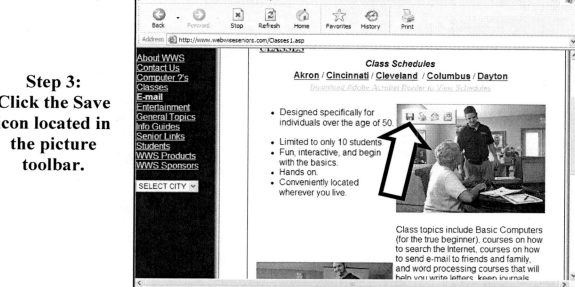

Step 3:
Click the Save icon located in the picture toolbar.

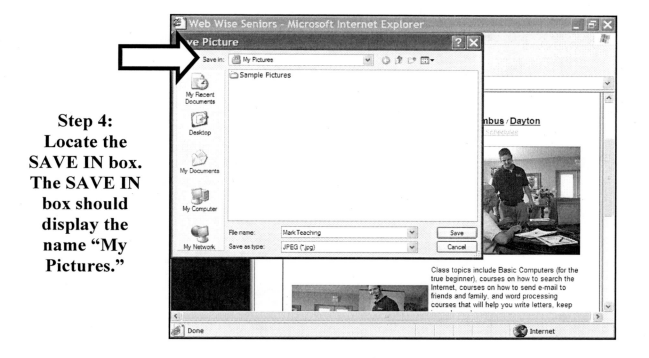

Step 4:
Locate the SAVE IN box. The SAVE IN box should display the name "My Pictures."

If My Pictures is not displayed in the SAVE IN box, click the gray arrow to open the drop down list.

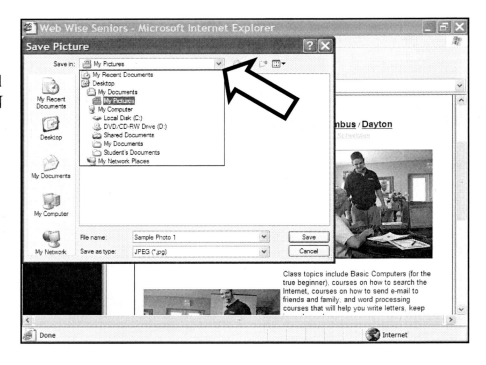

Click the "My Pictures" option.

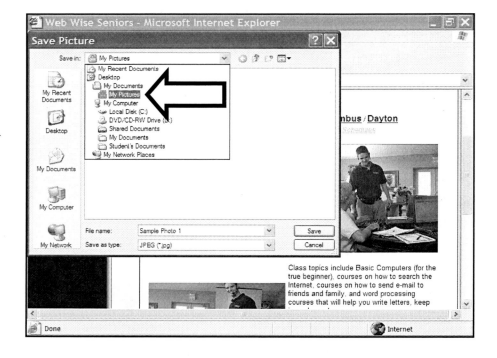

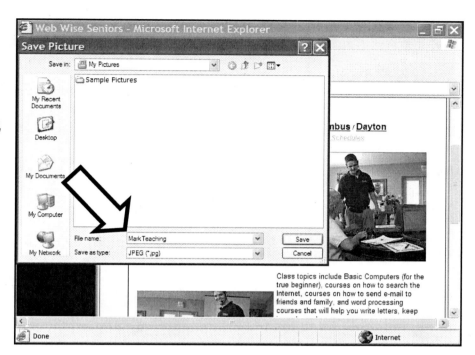

Step 5:
Locate the FILE NAME box and view the name of picture.

If you want to, rename the picture.

Click at the end of the current name.

Press the Backspace key on the keyboard.

Type in a new
name for the
picture.

Step 6:
Click the SAVE
button.

Chapter 13: Saving from the Internet!

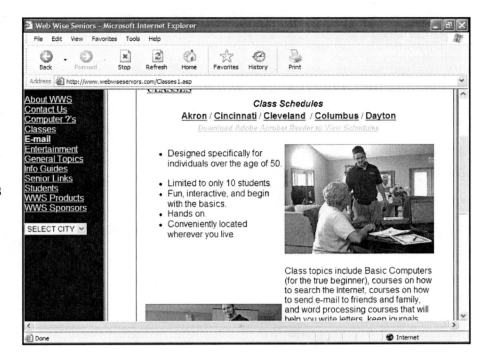

The image has been saved to the computer's main memory.

Saving Pictures (Using the Right Mouse Button): Step by Step Instructions

1. Find an image on the Internet.
2. Position the mouse over the image and click the RIGHT mouse button on the image.
3. Click the SAVE PICTURE AS option.
4. Locate the SAVE IN box. The SAVE IN box should display "My Pictures."
5. Locate the FILE NAME box and view the name of picture. Either leave the currently displayed name in the box or type in a new name.
6. Click the SAVE button.

Chapter 13: Saving from the Internet!

Saving Pictures (Using the Right Mouse Button):
Visual Guide

Step 1:
Find an image on the Internet.

Step 2:
Position the mouse over the image and click the RIGHT mouse button on the image.

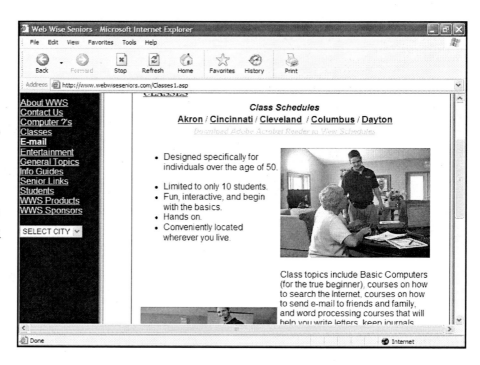

Step 3:
Click the SAVE PICTURE AS option.

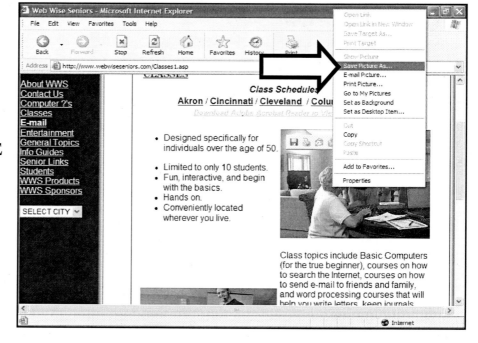

**Step 4:
Locate the
SAVE IN box.
The SAVE IN
box should
display the
name "My
Pictures."**

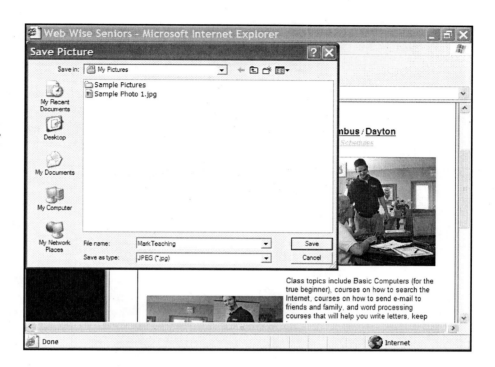

**You may want
to rename the
picture.**

**Click at the end
of the current
name.**

**Press the
Backspace key
on the
keyboard.**

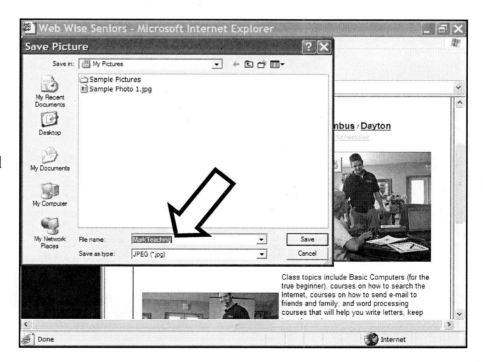

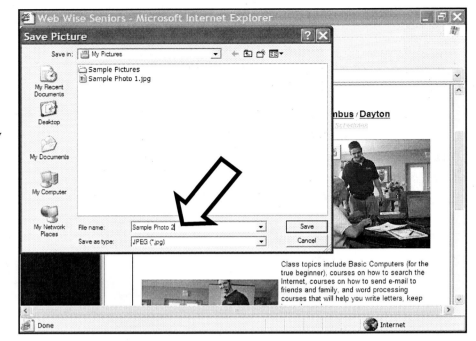

Type in the new name for the picture.

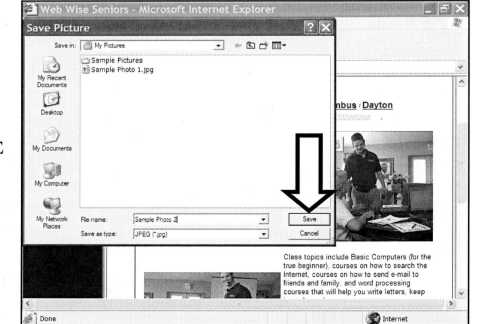

Step 5: Click the SAVE button.

The image has been saved to the computer's main memory.

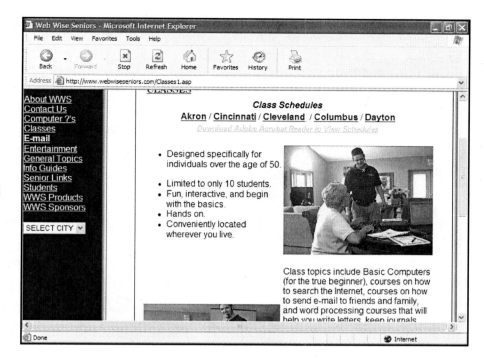

Once pictures have been saved, take a moment to verify they have been saved correctly. The pictures were saved into the My Pictures folder of the computer's hard drive. Access the My Pictures folder using the Start Menu.

Verifying the Pictures are Saved: Step by Step Instructions

1. Open the START Menu by clicking the START button.
2. Click the MY PICTURES option.
3. Locate the image name in the list provided.
4. Double-click on the icon representing the image listing. The picture should appear on your computer screen.
5. Click the CLOSE (X) button to exit the image.

Chapter 13: Saving from the Internet!

Verifying the Pictures are Saved: Visual Guide

**Step 1:
Click the
START button.**

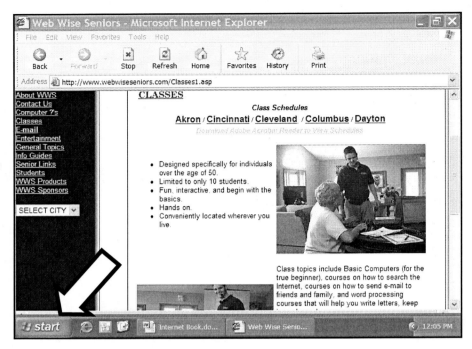

**Step 2:
Click the MY
PICTURES
option.**

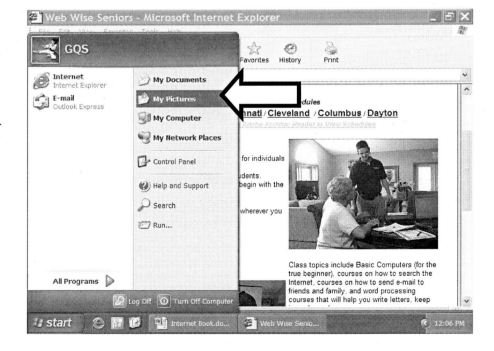

Step 3:
Locate the
image name in
the list
provided.

Step 4:
Double-click on
the icon
representing
the image
listing.

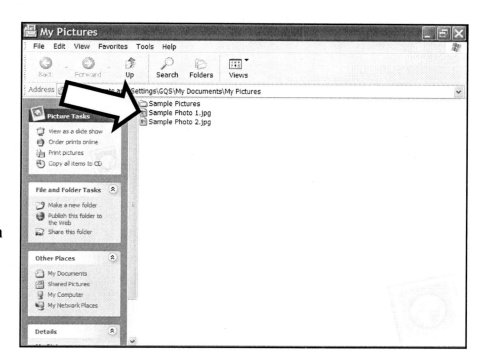

Click the
CLOSE (X)
button to exit
the image.

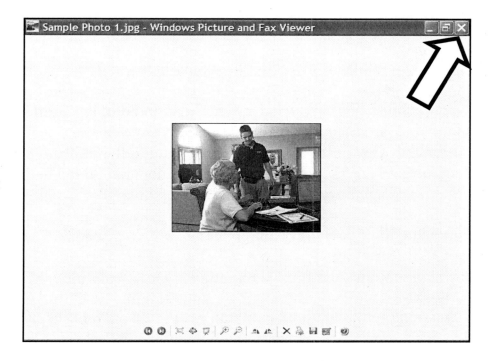

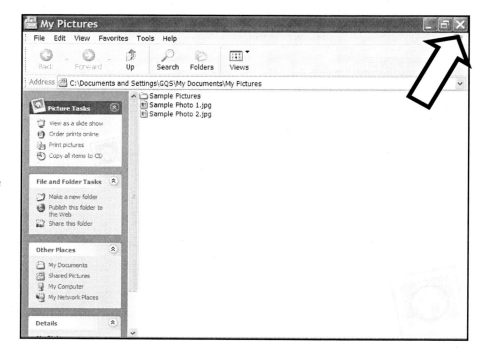

Click the CLOSE (X) button to close the MY PICTURES window.

Saving Text from the Internet

The next example will explain how to select a piece of text from a web page and save it. The process will use the concepts of highlighting, copying and pasting, and saving. Being able to save text from a web page without saving the whole page is a very useful tool.

Go back to the Web Wise Seniors Home Page. Locate and highlight the first four paragraphs. Once the text is highlighted, use the Edit menu to copy the text. After the text is copied, open a word processing program (e.g. Microsoft Word) and Paste the copied text into the new word processing document. Once the text has been pasted into the new document, save the document to the "My Documents" folder located on the computer's hard drive (main memory).

Let us begin. Open the browser screen and do a specific search for the Web Wise Seniors Home Page (www.webwiseseniors.com). Locate the address bar at the top of your browser window. Move your mouse pointer over any part of the white input box and click the left mouse button one time. Everything in the input box will turn blue. Use the backspace key or the delete key on the keyboard to erase the highlighted text. Begin typing the new website address (i.e. www.webwiseseniors.com). When you are finished typing, either hit the Enter key on your keyboard or click your left mouse button on the "Go" button located at the end of the address line. The web page will open.

Specific Search: Step by Step Instructions

1. **Obtain a website address.**
2. **Position the mouse pointer over the input box located in the address line.**
3. **Click the left mouse button one time.**
4. **Press the backspace key or the delete key on the keyboard to erase the highlighted text.**
5. **Type the new website address in the input box.**
    -   **Remember a website address typically includes:**
        o   **www. followed by**
        o   **The unique name, followed by**
        o   **The ending (.com , .gov , .net , .org , .edu or .cc)**
            ▪   **Example: www.WebWiseSeniors.com**
6. **Press the Enter Key on your keyboard to go to the website.**

Specific Search: Visual Guide

**Step 1:
Obtain a
website address.**

**Step 2:
Position the
mouse pointer
over the input
box located in
the address line.**

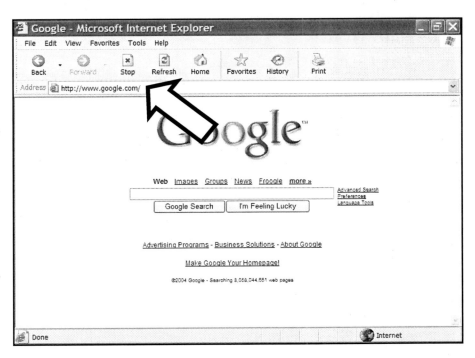

Step 3:
Click the left mouse button one time. The text in the line will turn blue.

Step 4:
Press the backspace key on the keyboard to erase the highlighted text.

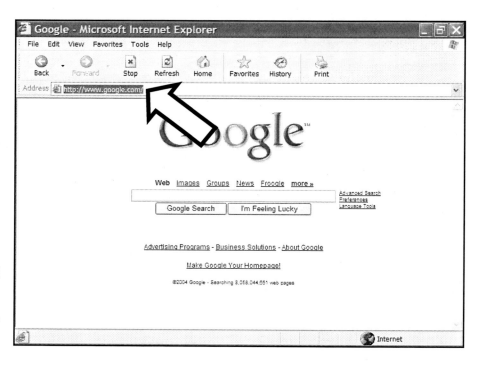

Step 5:
Type the new website address in the input box.

Step 6:
Press the Enter Key on your keyboard to go to the website.

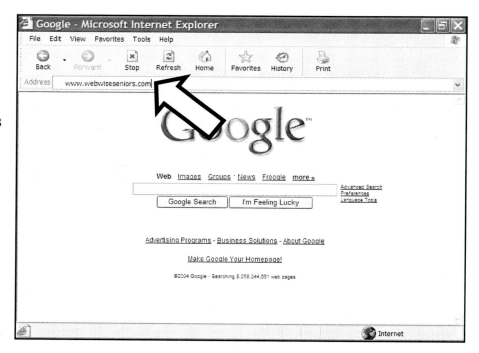

Chapter 13: Saving from the Internet!

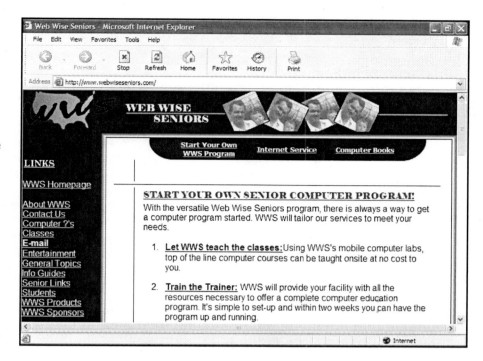

The Web Wise Seniors Home Page.

The next step is to highlight the first four paragraphs on the Web Wise Seniors Home Page.

Highlighting

Highlighting tells the computer what part of the web page you want to work with. To highlight text, position your mouse arrow at the end of the text you want to select. Click and HOLD DOWN the left mouse button. While holding down the mouse button, move your mouse arrow to the beginning of the selection. As the mouse moves over the text, it becomes highlighted (will have a black/blue background). After reaching the beginning of the desired text, release the mouse button. The selected text will remain highlighted. The computer is now ready to work with this selected text.

Highlighting Your Text: Step by Step Instructions

1. **Position the mouse at the end of the desired text.**
2. **Click and hold down the left mouse button.**
3. **Move the mouse to the beginning of the desired text.**
4. **Release the mouse button.**

Chapter 13: Saving from the Internet!

Highlighting Your Text: Visual Guide

The Web Wise Seniors Home Page.

Scroll down to locate the end of the fourth paragraph.

Step 1: Position the mouse at the end of the desired text.

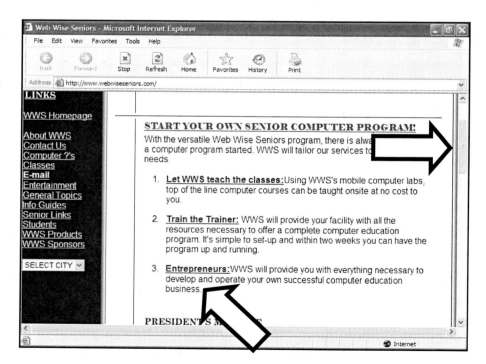

Chapter 13: Saving from the Internet!

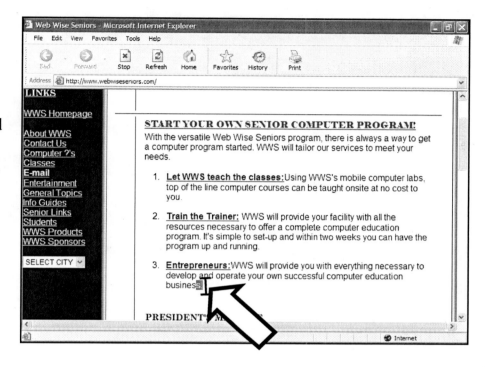

Step 2:
Click and hold down the left mouse button.

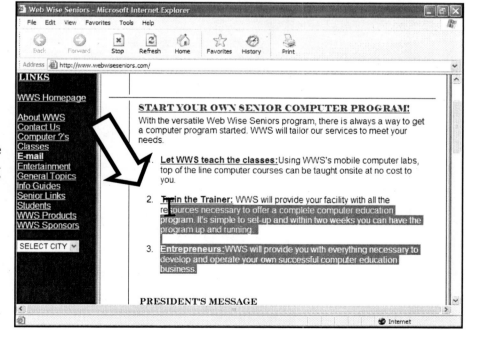

Step 3:
Move the mouse to the beginning of the desired text.

Step 3: (cont.)
Move the mouse
to the beginning
of the desired
text.

Step 4:
Release the
mouse button.

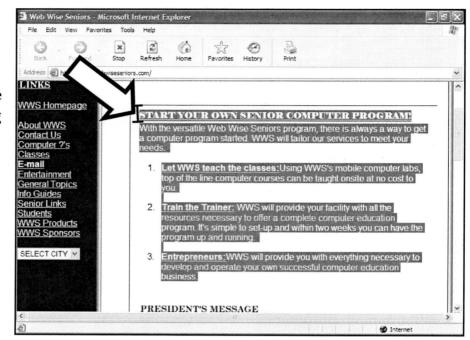

After the text is highlighted, you will be able to copy the text into the computer's temporary memory and then paste it into a new area. This is called copying and pasting.

Copying and Pasting

During the Copying and Pasting process, the computer places a copy of the highlighted text into a temporary holding area called the clipboard. Once you have opened the word processor, you can insert the text into the new document.

After the paragraphs have been highlighted, click on the Edit menu. Find and click on "Copy." The Edit menu will close. It will seem like nothing happened, but the computer has placed copy of the highlighted text into its temporary memory. Next open the word processing program and select the "paste" option located under the Edit menu of the word processing program.

Copying and Pasting: Step by Step Instructions

1. Highlight the text you want to copy.
2. Click on the EDIT menu.
3. Click the COPY option.
4. Open the word processing program and place your blinking cursor where you want the copied text to be located.
   a. Open the START menu.
   b. Click the ALL PROGRAMS option.
   c. Highlight the MICROSOFT OFFICE option.
   d. Click the MICROSOFT OFFICE WORD 2003 option. A blank piece of paper will open on your computer screen.
5. Click on the EDIT menu.
6. Click on the PASTE option.

Copying and Pasting: Visual Guide

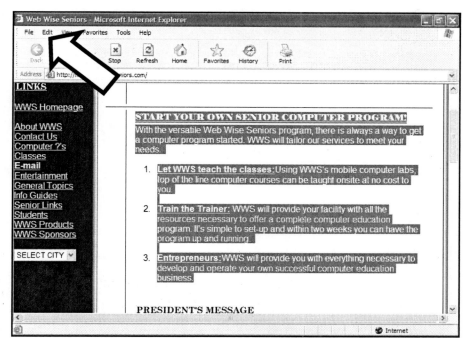

Step 1:
Highlight the text you want to copy.

Step 2:
Click on the EDIT menu.

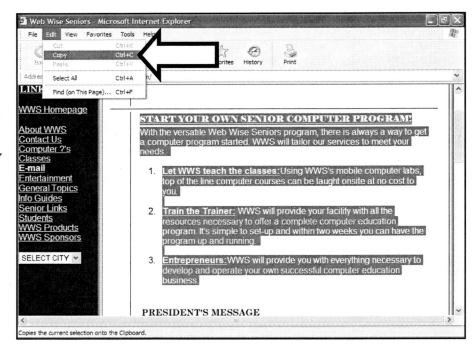

Step 3:
Click the COPY
option.

The text has been successfully copied to the computer clipboard.

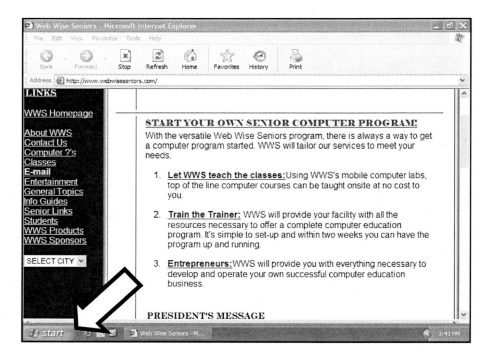

Step 4: Open
the Word
Processing
program and
paste the
highlighted
selection into
the Word
document.

Step a:
Open the
START Menu.

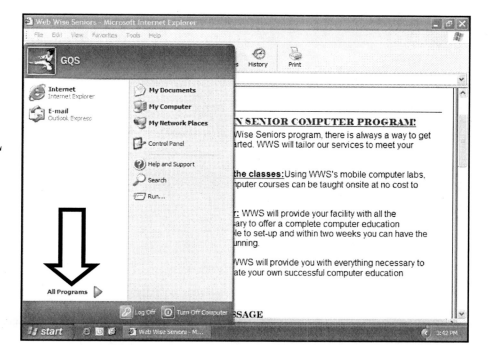

**Step b:
Click the ALL
PROGRAMS
option.**

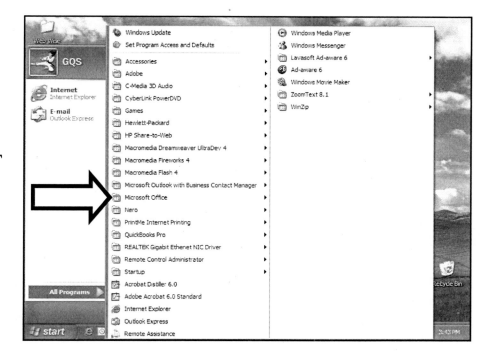

**Step c:
Highlight the
MICROSOFT
OFFICE
option.**

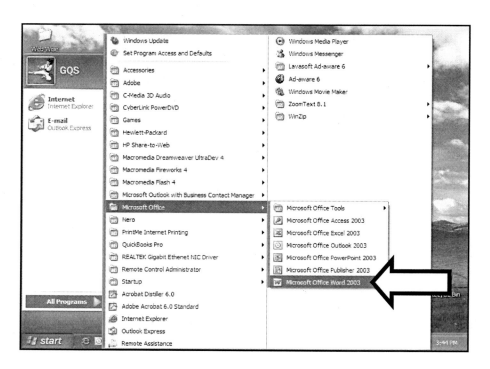

**Step d:
Click the
MICROSOFT
OFFICE
WORD 2003
option.**

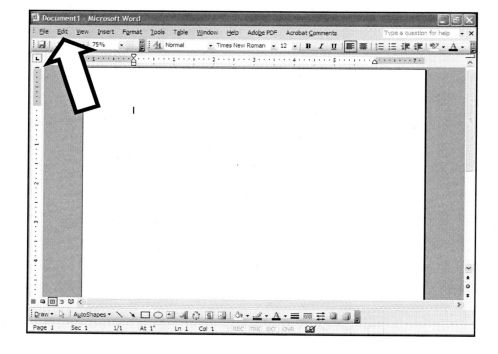

**Step 5:
Click on the
EDIT menu.**

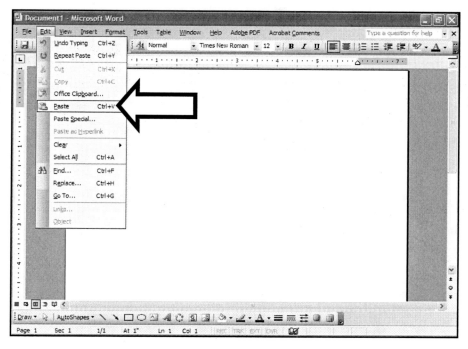

**Step 6:
Click the
PASTE option.**

**The text has
been pasted in
to the new,
blank Word
document.**

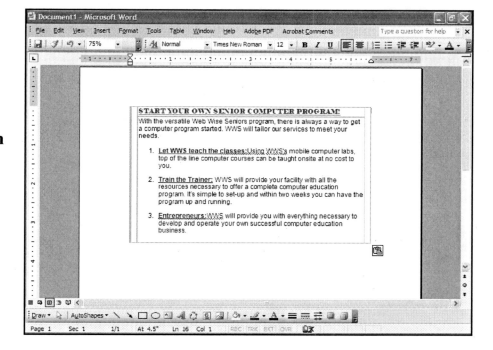

Chapter 13: Saving from the Internet!

Saving the Document

Once you have pasted the new text into the Word Document, you will need to save the document. Position the mouse arrow on the File menu located at the top of the browser window. Click the left mouse button once to open the menu. Move the mouse arrow down to the "SAVE AS" option and click the left mouse button. This will close the file menu and open the save screen. There are three additional steps to complete the save process. First, you must choose where to save the file. Second, you have to give the file a name. Third, you must click the save button.

Saving Your Work: Step by Step Instructions

1. Click on the FILE menu.
2. Click the option SAVE AS.
3. Locate the SAVE IN box and make sure My Documents is displayed.
4. Locate the FILE NAME box and type in the name of your document.
5. Click the SAVE button.

Chapter 13: Saving from the Internet!

Saving Your Work: Visual Guide

Step 1:
Click on the
FILE menu.

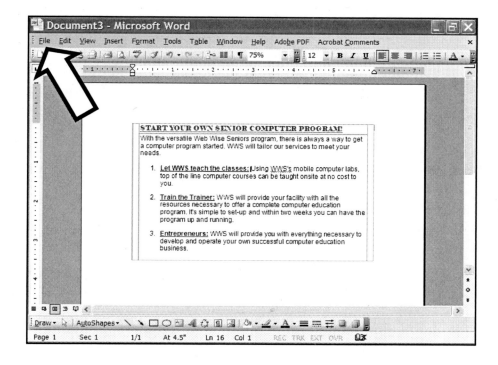

Step 2:
Click the option
SAVE AS.

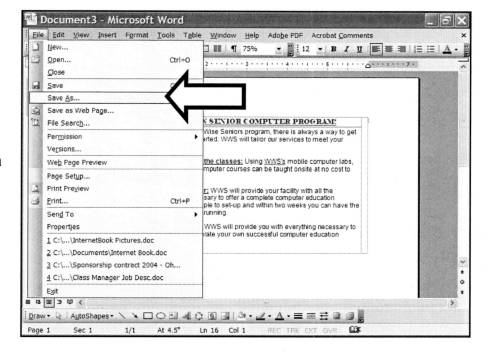

Step 3:
Locate the
SAVE IN box.
Make sure the
folder "My
Documents" is
displayed in the
box.

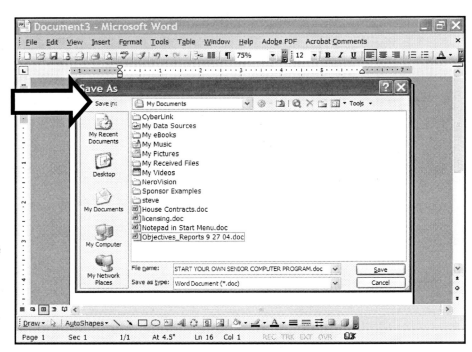

Step 4:
Locate the
FILE NAME
box and type in
the name of
your document.

File Name:
Text Example

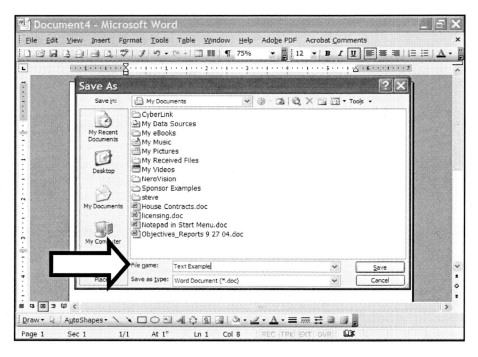

Step 5:
Click the SAVE button.

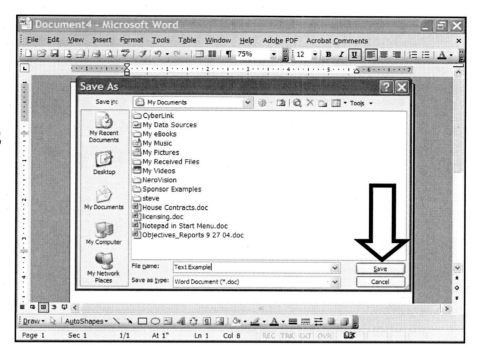

Successfully saved document.

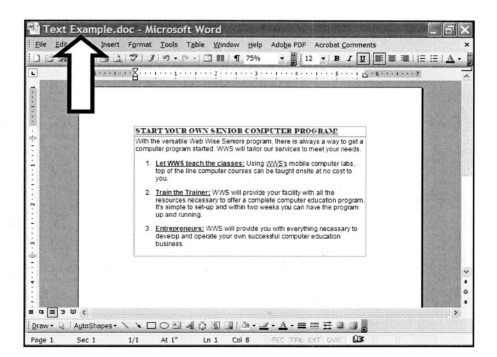

QUESTION: How do you know the file was saved successfully?

ANSWER: Look in the title bar of the program window (your document.) You will see the name of the document displayed in the title bar. This tells you the letter was saved correctly. In this example, the name in the title bar will have changed from "Document4" to "Text Example."

Chapter 14

Privacy on the Internet!

What You Will Learn in this Chapter
- ✓ How private is the Internet?
- ✓ Is it safe to purchase items on the Internet?

Section 32:   Internet Privacy

Think of your computer as a car for a moment. When you want to drive on the road, you have to go to the license bureau and get a license plate. Once your car has plates, you can drive freely on the road. The public does not know who you are, but can see the license plate. If a person wanted to attempt find out information about you, they would have to write down your license plate number and contact the license bureau. The license bureau will not disclose your personal information unless the person requesting the information is a member of law enforcement. So, to most people, you are just another car on the road represented by a license plate number.

The Internet is setup in a similar fashion. When you connect to the Internet, your ISP gives your computer a unique number called an IP address. This number distinguishes your computer from all of the others on the Internet. Your ISP is the only one who knows the number representing your computer. As an added bonus, every time you get connected, the ISP gives you a new number, making it even more difficult for others to track your Internet travels.

So, how does a hacker (information thief) get your information? The answer to this question relates to the information you have previously entered into your computer. When you first set up your computer, you were asked to type in your name. After the initial setup, other programs might have required additional information. For instance, a financial program might have requested the name of the bank you use and your account information. This information is stored in the computer's memory allowing the program to access it as needed. If the computer did not store the information, you would have to type the information in every time you used the financial program.

It is also common for websites to ask you to supply information about yourself. This enables the website to customize itself to better serve you. The website stores all this information on your computer in something called a cookie. The next time you go to the website, the website will look for this specific cookie as it loads the page. If the website finds its cookie, it will customize the page for you. Since all of this information is stored on your computer, if someone gets access to your computer, they can attempt to obtain your personal information. That is pretty scary.

So should we be worried? The answer is NOT REALLY. Even if a hacker intends to steal a person's information, the hacker does not know which computer is yours on the Internet. This means the hacker has to find you among the millions of people using the Internet at any one moment. In addition, your information is usually not worth the hassle. Most individuals do not have enough money, information, or power, to warrant the time it takes to steal their information and risk getting caught. Hackers usually target companies.

Why are companies' prime targets? First and foremost, they usually have a lot to lose. Also, many companies have websites which are available to the public. Each website is given a static (non-changing) IP address. A static address is necessary to allow the public access to the information stored on a company's website. Finally, most companies keep their computers connected to the Internet 24/7 (24 hours a day, 7 days a week) giving the hacker more time to try to break into the computer. Overall, hackers are looking for the big fish in the sea, not us minnows.

Buying Products and Services Online

Buying and selling products over the Internet is called E-commerce. Billions of dollars worth of transactions take place via the Internet every year. The U.S. Department of Commerce estimated U.S. retail e-commerce sales for the second quarter of 2004 was $15.7 billion, an increase of 23 % from one year ago.

Should we be worried when we purchase a product or service online? No, if you are careful to select reputable companies, identity theft should be of little concern. Websites conducting e-commerce use multiple layers of security, the most important of which is called data encryption. Most reputable merchants require a 128-bit Secure Socket Layer connection between the store and your computer browser. Basically this means that every piece of your information is encrypted using a 128-bit key before it is transmitted. It would take a hacker many years to try every possible combination to decipher the data. Most thieves do not want to waste their time getting one number; they want a large volume. Using your credit card online is no riskier than using it over a phone.

How can you be sure you are sending the information over a secure connection? The web browser has many ways of telling you an Internet connection is secure. The first signs of safety can be found in a browser's address bar. The address bar should display "https://" before the website address instead of just http://. You can also look at the bottom of your browser screen. A "padlock" is displayed in the browser status bar (lower right corner of the screen) when a secure connection is made. Finally, the browser will display a warning before you begin an information transfer which may not be secure. If you make sure to notice these signs, you can be relatively certain your information is safe.

Chapter 15

E-mail!

What You Will Learn in this Chapter

✓ What is e-mail?
✓ How do you select an e-mail provider?
✓ What makes up an e-mail address?
✓ How do you read e-mail?
✓ How do you write e-mail?

Chapter 15: E-mail!

Section 33: E-mail

E-mail has changed and continues to change the world in which we live. Electronic mail, also known as e-mail, enables people to communicate with others around the world instantly and at absolutely no charge. Whether you need to send a short note or a ten page letter, e-mail is your answer. With just a few quick steps, a message can be sent from your computer to anyone in the world.

E-mail's uses are nearly limitless. In the business world, e-mail is used to communicate with employees, advertise products, provide customer service, and more. On the social side, e-mail is used by relatives and friends, whether separated by only a few houses down the street or thousands of miles around the world, to keep in touch. As you can easily imagine, with such widespread use, e-mail has become the most popular aspect of the Internet. An estimated 80% of computer owners use e-mail to communicate.

Another great aspect of e-mail is that the system is not limited to text messages. E-mail enables users to send everything, from full-color photographs to important tax documents, just as quickly. With a couple clicks of the mouse, birthday pictures, tax returns, receipts, and even tickets purchased for concerts and sporting events can be sent and received within seconds.

The most amazing part of this is that you do not even need to own a computer to use e-mail. Many beginning computer users use their library's computers to access their e-mail. Other people use computers at schools, the homes of family and friends, businesses, or even local senior centers to access their e-mail accounts. As long as you can find a computer connected to the Internet, you can use e-mail.

Selecting an E-mail Provider
Once you are connected to the Internet, you need to decide what e-mail service provider you want to use. You have two basic options available. First, your Internet Service Provider will supply you with an e-mail account.

If you do not want to use your ISP's e-mail or if you just want a second e-mail address/account, there are many websites on the Internet which offer free e-mail service. Therefore, you can either use the e-mail account supplied by your ISP or sign-up for one of the many free e-mail services available on the Internet.

E-mail Addresses

Just as the United Postal Service requires everyone to have a unique mailing address to deliver mail, e-mail services require everyone to have a unique e-mail address. E-mail addresses, instead of being made up of street names, zip codes, and cities, are made up of sign-in names, @ symbols (pronounced AT), e-mail provider names, and Internet extensions such as .org, .com and .net. A typical e-mail address will look like Johndoe25@Hotmail.com. If you read the preceding e-mail address out loud, it would sound like "John Doe 25 at Hotmail dot com."

If you use your Internet Service Provider for e-mail, the username you selected during setup will be the first part of the e-mail address. After the username will be the @ (at) symbol followed by the ISP's name and extension.

Reading an E-mail Message

When you open your e-mail mailbox, called the inbox, the computer will provide a list of any received messages. The list will include who sent the message, the subject, date, and size of the message. From the list of messages, you can use the mouse to open a specific message.

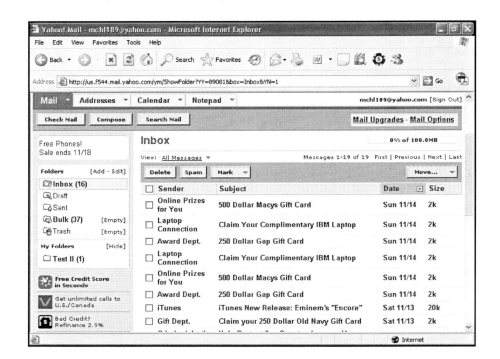

E-mail Inbox.

Once you have opened a message, it will appear in the read screen. Located at the top of the message is the "Message Header." The message header provides you with information about the message. The header includes who the message is FROM, the DATE the message was originally received, who the message was sent TO, and the SUBJECT of the message.

Below the header is the main message. The message can be a few words or a few pages in length depending on how much the sender wrote. After reading the message, you have the option to move to the next message in the mailbox, delete the current message, reply to the sender, or forward the message to someone else.

Reply - Sends a message back to the person who sent the message you are currently reading.

Reply All – Sends a message to everyone that received the message you are currently reading.

Forward – Sends the exact same message you are currently reading to another person.

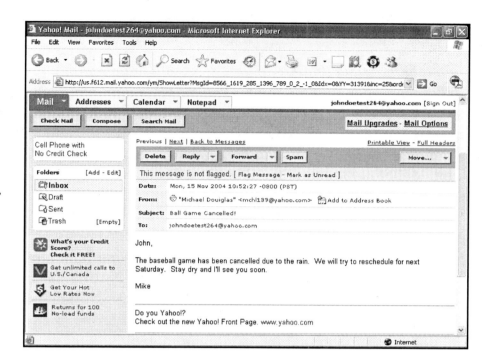

**E-mail
Read Screen.**

Writing an E-mail Message

If you want to compose and send an e-mail message, you can do that as well. Once you have told the computer you want to write a message, a screen will open, commonly called a compose screen, which will provide input boxes for each part of the new message. The compose screen has four main components including the TO: line, SUBJECT line, message box, and the SEND button.

The TO: line tells your e-mail service where to send your message. It works just like the delivery address on an "old fashioned" letter. Without the postal address, the post office cannot send your letter. Without an address in the TO: line, your e-mail system cannot send the e-mail message. You need to make sure you put in a person's entire e-mail address. This address goes in the TO: line, for example, JohnDoe25@Hotmail.com. Messages sent with partial or incorrect e-mail addresses will be returned.

Chapter 15: E-mail!

CAUTION: If an e-mail is returned to you and the e-mail address looks correct, check your "dots." It is very easy to accidentally insert a comma instead of a period, and it is very difficult to tell the difference. JohnDoe25@Hotmail,com looks very similar to JohnDoe25@Hotmail.com. Accidentally using a comma instead of a period is a very common mistake.

After inserting the e-mail address, click in the "SUBJECT" line to activate the blinking cursor and type in the subject of your message. The "SUBJECT" line is important because it provides the person receiving the message with an idea of what the message is about. For example, if you are sending a friend a message about your trip to Europe, a good subject would be "European Vacation."

The subject line of each message will be displayed in the receiver's inbox. A good, descriptive subject line will be appreciated by the receiver of the message. It helps to identify the contents of messages without forcing the reader to look at the entire message. Messages sent without subjects will automatically have "N/A" inserted in the subject line.

After filling in the To: line and the SUBJECT line, the next step is to write your text message. Every "New Message" screen will have a large white box near the middle or bottom of the screen. Click anywhere within this large white box to activate the blinking cursor. Type as much as you like. The message box will expand to fit long messages. A scroll bar will appear to help you move up and down through your message.

When you are finished typing the message, click the "SEND" button to distribute the message to the recipients.

We've given you the e-mail basics above. There is so much additional information relating to e-mail that we've published a book specifically to address e-mail.

Chapter 15: E-mail!

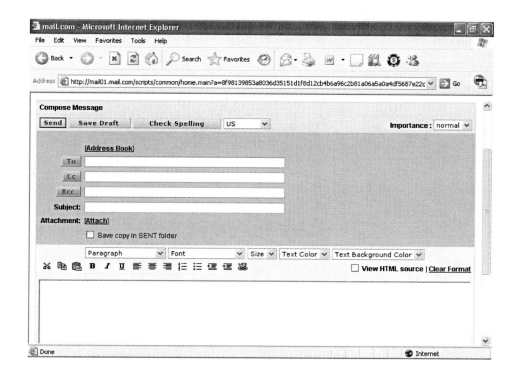

E-mail Compose Screen.

Chapter 15: E-mail!

Chapter 16

Internet Yellow Pages!

What You Will Learn in this Chapter
✓ What are some popular websites? (Note: Website addresses are subject to change without notice.)

Section 34:   Internet Yellow Pages

- **Anti–Virus**
    - MacAfee - www.mcafee.com
    - Norton - www.symantec.com

- **Auctions**
    - Amazon - auctions.amazon.com
    - Ebay - www.ebay.com
    - Yahoo - auctions.yahoo.com

- **Books**
    - Amazon - www.amazon.com
    - Barnes & Noble - www.barnesandnoble.com
    - Borders - www.borders.com

- **Computers**
    - Apple - www.apple.com
    - Dell - www.dell.com
    - Gateway - www.gateway.com
    - Sony - www.sony.com
    - Hewlett Packard - www.hp.com

- **Computer Training**
    - Web Wise Seniors - www.webwiseseniors.com

- **Electronics**
    - Best Buy - www.bestbuy.com
    - Circuit City - www.circuitcity.com

- **Employment**
    - Monster - www.monster.com

- **Financial**
  - Cbs.marketwatch - www.Cbs.marketwatch.com
  - American Stock Exchange (AMEX) - www.amex.com
  - Morningstar - www.Morningstar.com
  - Nasdaq Stock Market - www.nasdaq.com
  - New York Stock Exchange (NYSE) - www.nyse.com

- **Games**
  - Games - www.games.com
  - MSN Game Zone - zone.msn.com
  - Pogo - www.pogo.com
  - PopCap Games - www.popcap.com
  - Shockwave - www.shockwave.com
  - Yahoo! Games - games.yahoo.com

- **Greeting Cards**
  - 123greetings - www.123greetings.com
  - American Greetings - www.americangreetings.com
  - Blue Mountain - www.bluemountain.com
  - Hallmark - www.hallmark.com
  - Regards - www.regards.com

- **Home Improvement**
  - Home Depot - www.homedepot.com
  - Lowes - www.lowes.com

- **Instant Messenger Programs**
  - AOL - www.aol.com
  - MSN - www.msn.com
  - Yahoo - www.yahoo.com

- **Maps and Directions**
  - Expedia - www.expedia.com
  - Mapquest - www.mapquest.com
  - Yahoo Maps - maps.yahoo.com

- **Medical**
  - Eli Lilly - www.lilly.com
  - GlaxoSmithKline - us.gsk.com
  - Johnson & Johnson - www.jnj.com
  - Merck & Co. - www.merck.com
  - Pfizer - www.pfizer.com
  - WebMd - www.webmd.com

- **Movies**
  - Blockbuster - www.blockbuster.com
  - Hollywood Video - www.hollywoodvideo.com
  - Moviefone - www.moviefone.com
  - Movies.com - www.movies.com

- **Music**
  - Billboard - www.billboard.com
  - iTunes.com - www.itunes.com
  - MTV - www.mtv.com
  - VH1 - www.vh1.com

- **Newspapers**
  - Cleveland Plain Dealer -www.cleveland.com
  - Los Angeles Times - www.latimes.com
  - New York Times - www.nytimes.com
  - USA Today - www.usatoday.com
  - Washington Post - www.washingtonpost.com
  - Wall Street Journal - www.wsj.com

- **Search Engines**
  - AltaVista - www.altavista.com
  - Excite - www.excite.com
  - Google - www.google.com
  - Lycos - www.lycos.com
  - Yahoo – www.yahoo.com

- **Shopping**
  - Home Shopping Network - www.hsn.com
  - QVC - www.qvc.com
  - REI - ww.REI.com
  - Walmart - www.walmart.com

- **Software**
  - Adobe - www.adobe.com
  - QuickBooks/Quicken - www.intuit.com
  - Microsoft - www.microsoft.com
  - WinZip - www.winzip.com

- **Sports**
  - ESPN - espn.go.com
  - FOX Sports - www.foxsports.com
  - Sporting News.com - www.sportingnews.com
  - Yahoo! Sports - sports.yahoo.com

- **Travel**
  - CheapTickets - www.CheapTickets.com
  - Expedia - www.Expedia.com
  - Hotels - www.hotels.com
  - ORBITZ - www.ORBITZ.com
  - Priceline - www.priceline.com
  - Travelocity - www.travelocity.com

- **Toys**
  - KB Toys - www.kbtoys.com
  - Fisher-Price - www.fisherprice.com
  - Toys "R" Us - www.toysrus.com

- **Weather**
  - National Weather Service - www.nws.noaa.gov
  - Weather Channel - www.weather.com

- **White/Yellow Pages**
  - Verizon Super Pages - www.bigyellow.com
  - Yellow.com - www.yellow.com

Web Wise Seniors is Proud to Present...
Basic Computer Manuals for Beginners

These books are the absolute best instruction manuals for beginners. WWS answers all of the questions asked by real students in our classes. There is no better way to supplement what you have learned in class. Take the computer class home with you. Each manual is fully illustrated, providing step-by-step instructions in both written and picture format. Order your copy today!

BASIC COMPUTERS FOR BEGINNERS
Topics include:

- The Parts of the Computer
- How to use the Mouse
- Opening a Program using the Start Menu
- Turning the Computer On
- Saving Items
- Creating Folders
- Emptying the Recycle Bin
- Installing New Programs
- Using the Control Panel and Much More!!!!!!

BASIC WORD FOR BEGINNERS
Topics include:

- The Basics
- Short-cuts/Tricks
- Adding Pictures and Borders
- Cutting and Pasting
- Creating Columns
- Mail Merge
- Margins
- Printing
- Problem Solving and Much More!!!!!!

To Order Call Toll Free: 1-866-232-7032

Web Wise Seniors is Proud to Present...
Basic Computer Manuals for Beginners

THE INTERNET FOR BEGINNERS
Topics include:

- What can you Find on the Internet
- Selecting the Internet Service that's Right for You
- Comparing Cable, DSL and Dial-up
- Homepages and how to Change Them
- Understanding Browsers
- Using Web Addresses
- Surfing with Hyperlinks
- Search Engines
- Creating a Favorites List
- And Much More...

E-MAIL FOR BEGINNERS
Topics include:

- Selecting the E-mail Service that's Right for You
- What makes up an E-mail Address
- Avoiding Viruses & Junk Mail
- Sending E-mails
- Forwarding E-mails
- Reply vs. Reply All
- Keeping an Address Book
- Sending Attachments
- Opening Attachments
- And Much More...

To Order Call Toll Free: 1-866-232-7032

Thank you for using the Web Wise Seniors' Internet for Beginners book. We hope you enjoyed learning with it. Please let us know what you think of the book. If you found it easy to use and enjoyed the learning experience, please tell your family and friends.

Feel free to send your comments and feedback
to us at the following address:

Web Wise Seniors, Inc.
305 Woodstock Rd.
Eastlake, Ohio 44095

Or E-mail us at
WWS@WebWiseSeniors.com

Thank You!